INVESTORS' GUIDE FOR MAKING MEGABUCKS ON MERGERS

Other books by Richard J. Maturi

THE HOMETOWN INVESTOR

THE 105 BEST INVESTMENTS FOR THE 21ST CENTURY

STOCK PICKING: THE 11 BEST TACTICS FOR BEATING THE MARKET

MAIN STREET BEATS WALL STREET

DIVINING THE DOW

MONEY MAKING INVESTMENTS YOUR BROKER DOESN'T TELL YOU ABOUT

WALL STREET WORDS

Other books by Richard J. Maturi and Mary B. Maturi

WYOMING: OFF THE BEATEN PATH

CULTURAL GEMS: AN ECLECTIC LOOK AT UNIQUE UNITED STATES LIBRARIES

Investors' Guide for Making Megabucks on Mergers

How to Profit from Mergers, Acquisitions, Spin-offs, Stock Splits and Other Corporate Restructurings

Richard J. Maturi

21st Century Publishers

Library of Congress Catalog Card Number: 96-90004

Maturi, Richard J.
    Investors' Guide for Making MegaBucks on Mergers: How to Profit from
Mergers, Acquisitions, Spin-offs, Stock Splits and Other Corporate
Restructurings   /   Richard J. Maturi.
       p.   cm.
    Includes index.
    ISBN 0-9607298-2-8
    1.   Stocks.   2.   Investments—United States.   3.   Finance, Personal.
I.   Maturi, Richard J.   II.   Title: Investor's Guide for Making
MegaBucks on Mergers: How to Profit from Mergers, Acquisitions,
Spin-offs, Stock Splits and other Corporate Restructurings.

1 2 3 4 5 6 7 8 9 0

This publication is designed to provide accurate and authoritative information in
regard to the subject matter covered. It is sold with the understanding that the author
and the publisher are not engaged in rendering legal, accounting, or other professional service. If legal advice or other expert assistance is required, the services of
a competent professional person should be sought.

21st Century Publishers
1320 Curt Gowdy Drive
Cheyenne, Wyoming 82009
307-635-5511

Dedicated to individual investors with the gumption and savvy to make their own investment decisions and improve their portfolio performance.

Design by Seraph
Cheyenne, Wyoming

INVESTORS' GUIDE FOR MAKING MEGABUCKS ON MERGERS

Contents

Preface   xv

Acknowledgements   xvii

1. Mergers and Acquisitions   1

Mergers and Acquisitions   3

Record Mergers Create Exciting Investment Opportunities   3
The Mutual Fund Approach   7
Another Way to Tap Mutual Fund Expertise   18
Tracking the Acquirers   19
Industry and Stock Analysis   23
    Banking and Financial Services   23
    Health Care   38
    Industrial   46
    Natural Resources   55
    Telecommunications/Computers   64
Global Opportunities   76
Assessing Merger Candidate Characteristics   89

2. Turnarounds, Spin-Offs, Stock Splits & Buybacks   91

A. Tantalizing Turnarounds   93

Terrific Turnaround Profits   93
How to Recognize a Turnaround   96
Analyzing the Turnaround   99
Acquiring the Analysis Tools   103
Putnam's Pick   105
Turnarounds in the Making   107
Assessing Your Own Turnarounds   117

B. Successful Spin-Offs   119

Cashing in on Corporate Castoffs   119
Spin-Off Research   120
Searching Out Attractive Spin-Off Candidates   123
Analyzing the Orphans   127
Super Spin-Offs   130
Not All Spin-Offs are Made in Heaven   138
Specialized Spin-Off Information Sources   139

C. Stock Splits   141

The Stock Split Scenario   141
Stock Split Basics   142
Stock Split Realities & Theories   144
The Empirical Evidence   146
Where to Find Attractive Stock Split Candidates   149
Stock Split Prospects   153
Do Your Homework   160

D. Stock Buybacks   163

Record Stock Buybacks   163
Why Companies Repurchase Their Shares   165
Stock Buyback Research   167
Divining Buyback Candidates   169
Buyback Beauties   171

Special Discount Coupon   **178**

Glossary   **181**

Index   **193**

Investment Advertisement Offers   **196**

Preface

Institutional investors are making extraordinary profits in the midst of the biggest merger and acquisition boom this nation has ever seen. There are plenty of opportunities for the individual investor to participate in these significant investment gains by tracking the corporate restructuring of American and global companies.

Unlike the go-go years of the eighties when takeovers were financed by heavy debt loads and intricate financing that often lead to collapse, today's megamergers are driven by market economics and management's goal of creating more efficient, more profitable operations. As a result, companies emerging out of successful mergers are well-positioned to compete in the global economic arena, gain market share and increase revenues and profitability. As savvy investors recognize the new economic vitality and prospects of firms as a result of mergers, acquisitions and other corporate restructurings, they bid up the companies' stock prices.

Investors' Guide to Making MegaBucks on Mergers: How to Profit from Mergers, Acquisitions, Spin-offs, Stock Splits, and Other Corporate Restructurings shows the individual investor how to participate in the lucrative world of investing in mergers as companies vie to become competitively positioned for the 21st century.

You will learn how to analyze the impact of mergers and other corporate restructurings, how to ferret out potential acquisition candidates, where to obtain investment information on upcoming mergers, spin-offs, stock splits and other corporate activities and how to invest in these unique once-in-a-lifetime opportunities to enhance your portfolio returns significantly.

Don't let this golden opportunity pass you by. This book gives you the tools to tap into the information pipeline of one of the most lucrative investment environments in this century. As a bonus, you'll receive an analysis of key investments for consideration for your own portfolio. Join the big boys on Wall Street making MEGABUCKS on mergers.

Richard J. Maturi
Cheramie, Wyoming

Acknowledgements

I extend my thanks to the following who were kind enough to furnish research and charts to help make this book more informative and useful for investors: Babson-United Investment Advisors, Inc., Keith Brown, Ford Investor Services, Inc., David Ikenberry, James Miles, The New York Stock Exchange and Securities Data Company.

About the Author

Richard J. Maturi is a widely respected business and investment author whose more than 1,000 articles have appeared in such distinguished publications as *Barron's*, *Investor's Business Daily*, *Institutional Investor*, *Your Money*, *Industry Week*, *Kiplinger's Personal Finance*, *The New York Times*, *Your Company* and *Research*. In addition, he publishes three investment newsletters, *Utility and Energy Portfolio*, *Gaming and Investments Quarterly*, and *21st Century Investments* (See discount coupon offer in back of book).

Mr. Maturi is the author of *Wall Street Words* (Probus, 1991), *Stock Picking* (McGraw-Hill, 1993), *Divining the Dow* (Probus, 1993), *Money Making Investments Your Broker Doesn't tell You About* (Probus, 1994); *The 105 Best Investments for the 21st Century* (McGraw-Hill, 1995), *Main Street Beats Wall Street* (Probus, 1995) and *The Hometown Investor* (McGraw-Hill, 1996). Five of Maturi's books are Money Book Club selections.

Maturi is a member of the American Society of Journalists and Authors, Society of American Business Editors and Writers and the Denver Press Club. He attended the University of Notre Dame, received his Bachelor's degree from the University of Minnesota-Duluth and his M.B.A. from Oregon State University. While in the corporate world, he managed company pension and profit sharing funds and was a trustee on the Minnesota Teamsters Pension Fund. He and his wife, Mary, live in a log home in the Laramie Range of Wyoming's Rockies. Maturi has appeared on numerous radio and television interview shows including "Money Talk" on CNBC.

PART 1

Mergers and Acquisitions

Mergers and Acquisitions

Record Mergers Create Exciting Investment Opportunities

Without a doubt, 1995 proved to be a banner year for mergers and acquisitions in our nation's history. According to Securities Data Company, a Newark, N.J. firm that tracks merger activity, companies closed in on more than $458 billion in mergers and acquisitions during 1995, the biggest year on record. That amount topped the previous records of $347.5 billion in 1994 and the $335.8 billion recorded in 1988 during the frenzied days of debt-financed hostile takeovers. Overall, United States companies announced 8,954 merger and acquisition deals in 1995 compared with the previous high of 7,565 in 1994.

In contrast to the highly leveraged takeovers of the eighties, today's mergers and acquisitions are driven by market economics and management's desire to gain market share, increase efficiencies, trim costs and compete more effectively in the global economic environment.

"We're in the midst of a boom in merger and acquisition activity initiated by firms striving to achieve strategic objectives. While the financial sector has led the way, there has been a dramatic upturn in nonfinancial sector activity. The vast majority of mergers and acquisitions in the nineties are prompted by long-term strategic considerations as opposed to short-

3

term financial gains," says Frederick W. Green, president and co-portfolio manager of The Merger Fund.

The hot merger pace produced a record number of corporate name changes among New York Stock Exchange companies in 1995 when 60 name changes took place versus the previous record of 54 in 1994. Major reasons for today's mergers focus around long-term growth and enhanced competitive posture. Mergers and acquisitions often represent the easiest and least expensive way to enter new markets, acquire new products and/or technology and add new production capacity. With an economic slowdown poised on the horizon, mergers and acquisitions also represent a way for corporations to continue to expand their businesses and market share in the face of slower internal growth prospects.

The stock market rally over the past few years fuels the boom in mergers and acquisitions. With stock prices at record highs, companies have the "currency" to purchase other firms and operations without incurring a huge outlay of cash or taking on excessive debt levels.

Merger and acquisition activity has surged across the board. Just about every industry is experiencing some level of industry consolidation. In 1995, commercial banking accounted for 14.3 percent of all merger activity with $65 billion worth of combinations completed. Other industries with major merger and acquisition activity included food and beverage, manufacturing, pharmaceuticals, retail, telecommunications, transportation and utilities.

1995 was the year of the mega-merger with many of the corporate marriages exceeding $1 billion in value. Record making mergers begun or completed in 1995 included the combination of Chase Manhattan Corporation and Chemical Banking Corporation into a $10 billion financial force and the linking of Lockheed Corporation and Martin Marietta Corporation into the world's largest defense contractor, a $24 billion giant.

Investors in Chase Manhattan Corporation, Chemical Banking Corporation, Cordis Corporation, Dr. Pepper-Seven-Up Cos., First Fideltiy Bancorp, First Interstate Bancorp, Grow Group, Inc., John Labatt Ltd., Pratt & Lambert United Inc., Scott Paper and Surgical Care Affiliates and multitudes of other companies saw their share prices soar as mega-merger moves pushed up stock prices from nearly 20% to in excess of 60% in a period of days or weeks.

The trend is continuing with record mergers and acquisitions making headlines every day. Representative of mergers and acquisitions from across

4

the broad spectrum of industries include the proposed $1.8 billion take-over of Cordis Corporation by healthcare leader Johnson and Johnson Company, the $400 million acquisition of Pratt & Lambert United Inc. by paint industry leader Sherwin Williams Company, International Paper Company's $2.7 billion acquisition of Federal Paper Board Company, Inc. and the $11 billion bidding war between First Bank System Inc. and Wells Fargo & Company for First Interstate Bancorp.

Other merger activity included Campbell Soup Company's $1 billion acquisition of leading salsa maker Pace Foods Ltd., railroad giant Union Pacific Corporation's $1.2 billion purchase of Chicago & North Western Corporation and the $3.5 billion bid for Southern Pacific Rail Corporation and ITT Sheraton Corporation's purchase of Caesars World for $1.7 billion. ITT Sheraton's bid of $67.50 per share represented more than a 50% premium over the stock's then current trading price. It's a sure bet that Caesars World's shareholders rejoiced over their new-found fortune.

Merger mania extends beyond the boundaries of the United States as exhibited by the $2 billion takeover bids for John Labatt Ltd. (Canada) by Belgium's Interbrew SA and Canada's Onex Corporation and Quilmes Industrial S.A. of Luxembourg; the United Kingdom's Cadbury Schweppes $2.5 billion tender offer for Dr. Pepper/Seven-Up Cos. and interest in Scott Paper Company by United States companies Kimberly-Clark Corporation and Proctor & Gamble Company as well as British Unilever PLC to the tune of $7 billion.

Other international merger activity included a $1.3 billion bid for U.S. Shoe Corporation by Italy's Luxottica Group SpA; the $508 million purchase of Maybelline Inc. by French cosmetics leader L' Oreal SA; the $6 billion merger pact between U.S.-based Upjohn Company and Swedish Pharmacia AB; a move by Texas Utilities to acquire state-owned Australian electricity distributor Eastern Energy for $1.6 billion and Central & South West Corporation's $2.5 billion bid for U.K. utility Seaboard PLC.

While mergers and acquisitions typically imply a friendly environment for the combination of operations, takeovers represent an unfriendly bid by one company for another. In both events, companies seek to improve the bottom line through increased market share, cost reductions, operation synergies and the addition of complimentary product lines, distribution systems and markets.

However, some companies are more adept than others at putting together successful mergers and acquisitions. Likewise, some firms tend to pay too

5

much for an acquisition, especially when a bidding war for the target company results. According to one study of mergers and acquisitions between 1993 and late 1995, the acquiring company on average incurred a loss on the deal of 10%.

Even more importantly, investor perception of a bad deal can drive the acquirer's stock price down. Therefore, it's critical for the investor to understand the rationale behind a proposed merger or acquisition and the likelihood of the projected benefits and anticipated synergies coming to fruition. As mentioned earlier, a number of companies are savvy deal makers. Betting on the right horse can mean the difference between mediocre stock market gains or even a loss and significant investment returns from mergers and acquisitions.

Willard I. Zangwill, a professor at the University of Chicago's Business School, has studied the woes and performances of a number of acquirers to determine what makes a deal succeed or go sour. According to Zangwill, both successful and non-successful acquirers exhibit some identifying characteristics.

"The less successful acquirers strive heavily on how to make the deal, concentrating on the financial and legal aspects and often forgetting or giving little thought to what might happen after the purchase goes through. In contrast, the successful acquirer ferrets out and purchases only top firms and pays the right price to get the right company. These acquirers know that the acquisition price is not the key consideration. What drives the deal is the acquisition's potential after its purchase. Top performing firms acquire not necessarily to grow or employ idle cash, instead they desire to leverage special and unique knowledge and capabilities," says Zangwill.

Investigate how well past acquisitions have gone or determine if the companies or divisions have been sold off later at a loss. There is a big comfort factor in investing in acquiring companies which have pulled off successful deals in the past. That does not mean you should avoid investments in companies on the takeover path for the first time. However, you must perform some additional investigative work and analysis to assure yourself that management knows what it is getting into and is paying the right price for the proposed acquisition.

The Mutual Fund Approach

One way to tap into merger and acquisition activity is via the mutual fund route. You obtain professional management plus diversification. In addition, mutual funds can be purchased for a relatively small amount of money and built up over time. Another plus, many of the funds discussed below also invest in other unique opportunities discussed later such as spin-offs and turnaround situations.

THE MERGER FUND
100 Summit Lake Drive
Valhalla, NY 10595
Telephone: 800-343-8959
Ticker symbol: MERFX
Investment advisor: Westchester
    Capital Management, Inc.
Portfolio Co-managers: Frederick W.
    Green and Bonnie I. Smith

Year begun: 1989
Assets: $440 million
Minimum investment: $2000
IRA minimum: $2000
Load: None
Annual expense ratio: 1.41
Turnover: 200 percent
Morningstar rating: ★★★★

Investment Strategy. The Merger Fund attempts to capitalize on the explosion in mergers, takeovers, tender offers, leveraged buyouts, spin-offs, liquidations and other types of corporate reorganizations. The fund carries a Morningstar four star-rating and its risk levels rank lowest in its peer group for the three and five year performance periods. For calendar 1995 ended December 31, 1995, The Merger Fund showed a gain of 14.2 percent. In addition to its solid performance coupled with a low risk posture, the fund has never had a losing year under its advisor, Westchester Capital Management, Inc. of Valhalla, New York.

Returns

One-year	14.2 percent through 12-31-95
Three-year	12.9 percent through 12-31-95
Five-year	12.1 percent through 12-31-95

Representative Major Holdings (12/31/95)

Company	Industry
Midlantic Corporation	Banking
Capital Cities/ABC	Telecommunications/Broadcasting
Kemper Corporation	Insurance & Investment Mgt
Surgical Care Affiliates, Inc.	Healthcare
Cordis Corporation	Healthcare
Premier Bancorp	Banking
Bay Ridge Bancorp	Banking
Southern Pacific Rail Corp.	Transportation
First Interstate Bancorp	Banking
CBI Industries, Inc.	Industrial

Portfolio Composition. The Merger Fund makes between 100-200 investments, averaging around 50 announced deals in its portfolio at any one time. Positions are built up gradually as the proposed transaction moves through its life cycle. Financial services account for over 45% of the fund's assets, with telecommunications (12.4%), media (11.9%), technology (8.9%) and healthcare (7.2%) comprising other large positions.

Investment Assessment. The Merger Fund co-managers look for disparities between the current market price of a stock and its expected value at the conclusion of the deal and then analyze the potential annual return. Market inefficiencies and the inherent risk that the deal could fall through combine to create annualized returns ranging from 8% to more than 20%.

"We like to invest when the real risk is less than the risk perceived by the market. This takes research and an analysis of the strategic rationale for the merger (i.e. how motivated the parties are to complete the deal) and any regulatory approval issues. Many of these deals take many months or years to complete, so there's often no need to rush into a position," says Green.

The Merger Fund represents a safe harbor while providing attractive returns considering its low risk posture. The fund has both the lowest three-year risk rating and the smallest standard deviation among the more than 1,800 general equity funds tracked by Morningstar.

MUTUAL BEACON

51 J.F. Kennedy Parkway
Short Hills, NJ 07078-2702
Telephone: 800-553-3014
Ticker symbol: BEGRX
Investment advisor: Heine Securities
  Corporation
Portfolio manager: Michael F. Price

Year begun: 1985
Assets: $4.2 billion
Minimum investment: $5000
IRA minimum: $2000
Load: None
Annual expense ratio: .72
Turnover: 71 percent
Morningstar rating: ★★★★★

Investment Strategy. Mutual Beacon seeks capital appreciation with a secondary emphasis on income. The fund invests in common stock, preferred issues and corporate debt from a value perspective. It frequently invests in mergers with up to 50 percent of the portfolio assets in securities of companies involved in consolidations, liquidations, mergers, reorganizations and tender or exchange offers. Through proper analysis the fund tries to take advantage of the difference between perceived risk and actual risk. In recent years, the fund has moved into investment opportunities available in other areas of the world such as The Netherlands and Sweden.

Portfolio manager Michael Price seeks to identify companies whose assets are worth significantly more to a strategic acquirer than their value in the marketplace on a stand alone basis. Although the information contained here pertains specifically to the Mutual Beacon Fund, there are four value-oriented mutual funds under the Mutual Series umbrella. The other funds are the Mutual Discovery Fund, Mutual Qualified Fund and Mutual Shares Fund.

Returns

One-year	25.89 percent through 12/31/95
Three-year	17.79 percent through 12/31/95
Five-year	18.76 percent through 12/31/95

Representative Major Holdings (11/30/95)

Company	Industry
Chase Manhattan Corporation	Banking
RJR Nabisco Holdings Corp.	Consumer Products & Services

U S West, Inc.	Communications
Value Property Trust	Real Estate
Sprint Corporation	Communications
Philips Electronics NV	Conglomerates
Tenet Healthcare Corp.	Healthcare
MSCW Investors	Real Estate
Volvo AB	Industrial
Getinge Industrier AB	Healthcare

Portfolio Composition. The Mutual Beacon Fund possesses a well-diversified portfolio with approximately 8.4% of its portfolio in banking issues, 7.1% in retail, 6.6% in healthcare, 5.4% in communications, 5.0% in conglomerates, 4.8% in insurance, 4.4% in food and beverages and 4.2% in industrial. Other major portfolio asset categories include aerospace, consumer products and services, entertainment and media, financial services, natural resources, printing and publishing and the securities industry. As of November 30, 1995, common stocks accounted for over 69% of the portfolio while cash (22.5%), bonds (6.6%) and preferred securities (1.5%) made up the balance.

Price has taken a more active stance in overseas investments in recent years with a variety of Dutch, Swedish and other European firms comprising over 20% of the portfolio assets. On average; Price combines 8% bankruptcies, 10% mergers and acquisitions, 60% in cheap stocks with a 22% cash position.

Investment Assessment. Mutual Beacon and other Mutual Series Funds earned over $360 million for their shareholders on positions in Chase Manhattan and Chemical Bank. Chase traded at $35 per share despite a book value around $40 per share. In addition, it was earning $5 per share and possessed a nice banking franchise.

"Chase was much too cheap. With that kind of underlying value there was minimum downside risk," says Price.

Another major contributor to profits was Mutual Beacon's investment in Columbia Gas System, Inc. the fund's largest single bankruptcy investment.

Michael Price, chairman, president and chief operating officer of Mutual Beacon's investment advisor Heine Securities Corporation, special-

10

izes in purchasing $1 worth of assets for 50 cents. For the one-year period ended December 31, 1995 Mutual Beacon earned a return of 25.9 percent.

"We don't have the ability to predict earnings growth so we concentrate on discovering asset values that are not recognized by the market and are trading at a discount to their true value. Among the analysis yardsticks used by Price's team are multiples of cash flow and replacement value. Undervaluation can come about for many reasons, including bad publicity.

Take Archer-Daniels-Midland Company for example. Price liked the company because the stock dropped from $20 per share to $16 per share in the wake of price fixing investigations. With 500 million outstanding shares the stock price drop translates to $2 billion in lost market value.

"There's no way that the problem will be that big," says Price.

Another value play in the takeover news that Price favored was Chrysler Corporation. With $7 billion in cash and virtually no long-term debt there was an underlying value of nearly $20 per share in cash to support the price level around $48 per share.

Looking ahead, Price sees opportunities in the beat up retail sector, trucking industry and oil and gas. Service Merchandise Company, Inc. is the nation's largest catalog showroom merchandiser and is in the midst of a turnaround with rising gross margins and a refined marketing strategy. Landstar System operates the third largest truckload carrier business in North America and stands to benefit from an economic upturn and further increased commerce between the United States and Canada and Mexico under NAFTA. Canada's Imperial Oil Limited (owned nearly 70 percent by Exxon Corporation) boosted earnings on its best petrochemical sector performance ever and rising heavy oil prices. A strong cash flow position, stock buyback program and cost cutting efforts are all benefits.

Price will continue to search out value situations in the world of mergers and acquisitions and other corporate restructurings.

J. HANCOCK REGL BANK FD B

101 Huntington Avenue
Boston, MA 02199-7603
Telephone: 800-225-5291
Ticker symbol: FRBFX
Investment advisor: John Hancock
   Advisors
Portfolio manager: James Schmidt

Year begun: 1985
Assets: $1.4 billion
Minimum investment: $1000
IRA minimum: $500
Load: Up to 5%
Annual expense ratio: 2.06%
Turnover: 13%
Morningstar rating: ★★★★★

Investment Strategy. The John Hancock Regional Bank Fund Class B strives to achieve capital appreciation with a secondary emphasis on income. Portfolio Manager John Schmidt anticipates the continuing consolidation of the banking industry. From over 14,000 banks competing for business in 1985, the number dropped to 11,200 by 1993 and is projected to decline even further to approximately 4,000 banks by the year 2010.

Schmidt actively seeks stocks that may benefit from mergers and acquisitions. Other investment criteria include the existence of strong management, undervalued situations and a history of solid profitability without undertaking undue risks.

Returns

One-year	47.56 percent through 12/31/95
Three-year	21.08 percent through 12/31/95
Five-year	33.78 percent through 12/31/95

Representative Major Holdings (12/31/95)

Company	Region
First Interstate Bancorp	West
PNC Financial Corporation	Northeast
Greenpoint Financial Corp.	Northeast
First American Corporation	Southeast
Fleet Financial Group Inc.	East
First Tennessee National Corp.	Southeast
Bank of New York Company	Northeast
Mercantile Bancorporation	Midwest
First of America Bank Corp.	Midwest
BankAmerica Corporation	West

Portfolio Composition. As its name implies, The John Hancock Regional Bank Fund Class B invests in regional banks but also has stakes in various financial services companies, institutions with substantial lending operations and large money-center banks with international connections. The

12

fund's major goal is capital appreciation with a secondary interest in income.

Approximately 65% of portfolio assets are invested in equity securities, up to 5% may be invested in a combination of below-investment grade debt securities of banks and non-financial services equities and up to 15% percent of net assets may be invested in short-term investment grade debt securities of corporations, certificates of deposit or obligations of the United States Government. The portfolio is well-diversified with over two hundred different securities.

The portfolio breakdown by region is headed by the Northeast with 33% and followed by Southeast (27%), Midwest (23%), West (16%) and Southwest (1%).

Investment Assessment. The John Hancock Regional Bank Fund Class B has outperformed both the NASDAQ Bank Index and Lipper Financial Services Average benchmarks for the one-year, five-year and since inception (1985) time frames. Without a doubt, the banking industry consolidation will continue unabated well into the next century. There will be ample opportunities for substantial capital gains investing in takeover targets and acquiring companies well positioned to garner market share in the banking and financial services industries during the years ahead.

Schmidt has proven his ability to deliver superior returns over the long-term. This fund represents a below average risk way to achieve higher returns in the banking merger and acquisition game.

CENTURY SHARES TRUST

One Liberty Square
Boston, MA 02109
Telephone: 800-321-1928
Ticker symbol: CENSX
Investment advisor: Century Capital
  Management, Inc.
Portfolio manager: Allan W. Fulkerson

Year begun: 1928
Assets: $267 million
Minimum investment: $500
IRA minimum: $500
Load: None
Annual expense ratio: 0.94%
Turnover: 5%
Morningstar rating: ★★★

Investment Strategy. Century Shares Trust applies a long-term strategy of capital gains through a diversified portfolio of common stocks or securities convertible into the common stock of banks, insurance companies, insurance brokers and other firms providing services to, or closely related to, banks and insurance companies. Taking a different tact to most other financial services sector funds, Century Shares Trust has held predominantly securities of insurance companies for the past several years. The long-term holding strategy results in a relatively low turnover rate and lower associated expenses.

Returns

One-year	35.23 percent through 12/31/95
Three-year	9.00 percent through 12/31/95
Five-year	16.68 percent through 12/31/95

Representative Major Holdings (9/30/95)

Company	Industry
General Re Corp.	Insurance
American Intl Group, Inc.	Insurance
St. Paul Companies, Inc.	Insurance
AON Corp.	Insurance
MBIA Inc.	Insurance
The Chubb Corp.	Insurance
The Progressive Corp.	Insurance
Cincinnati Financial Corporation	Insurance
SAFECO Corp.	Insurance
Ohio Casualty Corp.	Insurance

Portfolio Composition. As indicated above, Century Shares Trust maintains a heavy weighting of insurance stocks, nearly 89% of its portfolio assets. Banking stocks comprise a little over 5% of portfolio assets, mainly concentrated in J.P. Morgan & Company, Inc. and Wachovia Corporation shares. Common stocks account for 93% of the assets with the balance consisting of convertible securities, United States Treasury Notes and cash equivalents. Portfolio manager Fulkerson invests in high quality companies with top management.

Investment Assessment. Just as we will investigate turnaround companies in Part 2, Century Shares Trust represents a turnaround in the making in the mutual fund industry. Despite solid long-term performance and gains of 31 1/2% and 27% in 1991 and 1992 respectively, Century Shares Trust stumbled in 1993 and 1994 with declines of 0.4% and 3.9% before rebounding strongly in 1995 with a return in excess of 35%.

Fulkerson's assessment that the insurance industry is undergoing significant changes and facing major challenges and that quality management will come out on top drives his investment strategy.

With the fund's portfolio trading at less than twelve times projected 1996 earnings, Century Shares Trust trades at a significant discount to the S & P 500. An appropriate and interesting investment vehicle for conservative investors wishing to take a defensive stance in today's lofty market prices. Over the long term the fund's current portfolio has produced an average annual compound growth of book value plus dividends totaling 19.1%, more than 80% greater than that achieved by the S & P 500.

THIRD AVENUE VALUE FD, INC.

767 Third Avenue, Fifth Floor
New York, NY 10017-2023
Telephone: 800-443-1021
Ticker symbol: TAVFX
Investment advisor: EQSF Advisers, Inc.
Portfolio manager: Martin J. Whitman

Year begun: 1990
Assets: $440 million
Minimum investment: $1000
IRA minimum: $500
Load: None
Annual expense ratio: 1.15%
Turnover: 5%
Morningstar rating: ★★★★★

Investment Strategy. The Third Avenue Value Fund pursues long-term capital appreciation by investing in the undervalued securities of well-capitalized companies. Unlike many high-turnover funds, Third Avenue Value follows a disciplined buy and hold strategy. Turnover can run as high as 67% as experienced in the fund's debut year of 1990 to as low as the 5% turnover rate of 1994.

Portfolio manager Martin J. Whitman often avoids the beaten path, investing in distressed securities and industries and relatively inactive markets.

"We don't try to market time or pay attention to prices quoted for stocks and bonds held in our portfolio. We look strictly to the performance of the businesses and the resources of those businesses we hold. We attempt to

15

achieve superior performance by avoiding investment losses rather than trying to predict the future. We buy what is both "safe" and "cheap" according to our investment criteria, with a primary emphasis on "safe." We purchase the common stocks of companies with high quality financial positions," says Whitman.

Whitman invests in undervalued situations based on the long-term outlook for the company, the ability to finance the transaction and appropriate exit strategies. Third Avenue Value Fund generally does not pay more than 80% of pro-forma book value for well-capitalized depository institutions or more than 160% of book value for venture capital situations. In the real-estate, broker/dealer, financial insurance and title insurance equities sectors, the Third Avenue Value Fund ignores book values and places its emphasis on either appraised values or estimated sales values. It looks at the price of a common stock against what the company would be worth as a private business or as a takeover candidate.

"We don't look at the big picture such as interest rates and the political environment, that's strictly for amateurs. We look at the value of the company and purchase its common stock usually before catalysts such as merger proposals surface," says Whitman.

Returns

One-year	30.41 percent through 11/30/95
Three-year	18.69 percent through 11/30/95
Five-year	23.27 percent through 11/30/95

Representative Major Holdings   (11/30/95)

Company	Industry
Eljer Industries, Inc. (Bank debt)	Building Products
Raymond James Financial, Inc.	Security Brokers, Dealers
First American Financial Corp.	Title Insurance
Digital Equipment Corp.	Computers, Office Equipment
Capital Guaranty	Financial Insurance
MBIA, Inc.	Financial Insurance
Sun America Inc.	Insurance
Stewart Information Services	Title Insurance

Portfolio Composition. The Third Avenue Value Fund maintains a heavy weighting in financial insurance securities with 10.7% of its portfolio assets from that sector. Other major positions include investments in security brokers (9.3%), venture capital (8.4%), title insurance (5.7%) and computer and office equipment (5.0%). Recent portfolio composition consisted of nearly 70% stocks, 10% bonds and 20% cash.

Investment Assessment. The Third Avenue Value Fund has delivered solid, consistent performance since its inception in late 1990. Whitman dove into the derivative market head first as other investors avoided them like the plaque. As a result, Whitman picked up inverse floaters at a huge 55% discount. Now those investments are delivering a solid 10% to 12% yield to maturity. The fund's regional broker-dealer position in Raymond James Financial, Inc. is up over 50% since its acquisition in early 1994. Whitman used Raymond James Financial as an LBO case study at Yale University and the analysis showed the company would be a steal at $25 per share. Incidentally, Third Avenue Value Fund purchased its Raymond James Financial position at an average cost of $14 per share.

Likewise, as other investors shunned Piper Jaffray, Whitman chalked up a better than 20% gain through November, 1995. Overall, the Third Avenue Value Fund ranks in the top third of its Morningstar benchmark group for 1995 and over the five years of its existence through October 31, 1995 ranks in the top 3% of equity or balanced mutual funds, on a load-adjusted basis. In the wake of the Orange County debacle, Whitman purchased exceptionally well-financed companies in the financial insurance industry at less than ten times 1994 earnings. With much of the U.S. infrastructure crumbling, he believes there's good reason for taking a stake in financial insurance firms which will serve the municipal bond market with an anticipated rising volume of new muni offerings in the years just ahead.

"Competition from new entrants into the financial insurance industry is likely to be limited due to the need to be able to deliver AAA ratings to bondholders. Companies like MBIA are likely to benefit in this situation," says Whitman.

Looking to the future, Whitman finds undervaluation in the closed-end fund arena.

17

"Closed-end funds represent the largest pools of unencumbered liquid capital in the free world. With investor dissatisfaction in closed-end funds and subsequent wide discounts, these funds represent prime takeover targets," says Whitman.

Look for Third Avenue Value to continue to deliver impressive performance based on purchasing equities of companies with strong financial positions, responsible management and a market price no more than 50% of estimated private business asset value. On the fixed income front, Third Avenue Value Fund purchases debt securities with strong protective convenants and a yield to maturity of at least 500 basis points above comparable yields.

To down play fears of losing the captain of the fund with Whitman recently turning age 71, Whitman is supported by a research staff of twenty investment bankers, analysts and other professionals. Two of the Third Value Fund's senior analysts are in the running to replace Whitman as portfolio manager, but not until he's ready to turn over the helm...and that's not likely to happen anytime soon.

Another Way to Tap Mutual Fund Expertise

You can tap the expertise of professional portfolio managers without purchasing the funds themselves. First, call the 800 toll-free numbers of mutual funds investing in the sectors you are interested in and request a copy of their most recent quarterly or semi-annual reports.

Second, study their portfolio holdings paying particular attention to increases and decreases in positions in order to determine market trends. Third, invest in the securities which fit your investment objectives and risk posture.

The annual, semi-annual and quarterly reports of mutual funds represent a gold mine of information and investment opportunities. For example, according to Whitman of the Third Avenue Value Fund (see earlier discussion) many of his fund's holdings become takeover targets years down the road after other investors and companies recognize the undervalued situations.

The following companies involved in recent mergers or announced mergers or takeovers were gleaned from a combination of perusing the holdings of mutual fund companies such as those above and tracking the merger and acquisition arena as it plays itself out in the financial press and business publications such as *Barron's, Forbes, Fortune, Industry Week, Investor's Business Daily, The Wall Street Journal* and *Your Money*. In addition, you can more closely follow how merger deals are coming together and their impact by keeping yourself updated with specialized publications covering this area such as the weekly *Mergers and Acquisitions Report* published by Investor's Dealers' Digest in New York City.

Tracking the Acquirers

Securities and Exchange Commission regulations require that whenever an entity purchases 5 percent or more of any class of a company's securities, a Schedule 13D report must be filed with the SEC within ten days. In addition, any subsequent change in holdings or intentions must be reported to the SEC on an amended filing. Keeping posted on potential takeovers by tracking 13D activity makes sense and can help position you to take advantage of stock price spurts before they happen.

Barron's and other financial publications regularly report on 13Ds filed with the SEC. Periodically reviewing these listings can give you a pulse for the merger and takeover market. While increases in holdings can signal potential takeover targets, decreases in holdings may represent an early sign of the cooling off of interest in a particular company or industry segment.

For example, filings in January and March 1995 reflected a backing off of investor interest in the gaming sector. FMR Corporation disposed of 364,072 shares of Bally's Grand between November 3 and December 28, 1994 while PAR Investment partners sold off 520,000 shares of Bally Gaming International between February 6 to March 3, 1995. On the other hand, interest in banking and financial services companies continued to heat up in early 1995 as Gibraltor Holdings increased its stake in CVD Financial to 444,300 shares (22.5%) in late December 1994 and early January 1995. Also Josiah Austin and others raised their stake in New York Bancorp to 1,076,339 shares (7.95) between late January 1995 and late February 1995.

More recently, the following 13D filings showed interest in a wide variety of industries such as financial services, telecommunications, transportation and water utilities.

— A group including James J. Cramer increased its holdings in Westerfield Financial to 447,100 shares (9.9%) with the acquisition of 69,100 shares from December 14, 1995 to January 17, 1996 at prices ranging from $16.30 to $16.69 per share.

— Gamco Investors et al. purchased a net 112,000 Class A shares of Cablevision Systems at a cost of $46.80 to $55.89 per share from December 28, 1995 and January 15, 1996. This raised Gamco's holdings to 969,194 shares (7.79%).

— FMR Corporation was active again, this time purchasing 846,000 shares of US Air Group between December 27, 1995 and January 4, 1996 at prices ranging from $13.25 to $14.38 per share. Its stake in US Air Group rose to 6,620,259 shares (10.45%).

— James Harpel et al. bought 34,800 Western Water shares over a sixty day period prior to February 5, 1996. The acquisition cost was $29.50 to $30.50 per share. The group raised its stake to 226,600 shares (5.73%).

These investors purchase the stocks for one reason. They consider the share prices undervalued by the market and hope to capitalize on this disparity between the company's underlying value and its current stock price. The investors can earn exceptional investment returns in several ways. First, they can take over the company and sell or spin-off divisions of the company for prices greater than they paid for the entire company. Second they can purchase the company and operate it more efficiently than the present management. Third, they can purchase the undervalued shares and sell them later at a higher price after the market realizes the company's real potential. Finally, they can attempt a takeover and sell the shares back to the target company or a "white knight" at substantially higher prices.

Research by professors Wayne Mikkelson of the University of Oregon and Richard Ruback at the Massachusetts Institute of Technology tracked 473 initial Schedule 13D filings by corporations over a three year period from 1978 through 1980. Mikkelson and Ruback found that 206 of the initial investments or 44 percent preceded some form of completed takeover within three years. Company repurchases accounted for 40 or 8 percent of the final outcome.

More importantly, Mikkelson and Ruback tracked the stock performance of the target companies from the initial Schedule 13D filing. They determined that all shareholders in these firms achieved abnormal above-average returns for each type of final outcome within the three year period. However, the stock of target companies in situations with no outcome within the three-year period decreased in value on average for investors who held onto their shares throughout the three-year period. Investors who sold during the three-year period made abnormal positive returns despite no final outcome.

Obviously, as mentioned earlier by The Merger Fund's Green, "It's important to assess the desire and ability of the parties to carry through the merger or takeover." Likewise, it is critical for your investment return to know when to sell your stake in a takeover target. Since the study only covered a three-year period, it's possible that those investors who held onto their shares beyond the three years may have made money in the long-term if the company and its stock price turned around after the three-year research time period.

Schedule 13D filings that indicate plans to takeover another company provide the greatest indication that a takeover is indeed in the works. You have to be careful, however, not to chase the stock and pay too high a premium for takeovers in the late stages. You want to ride the price rise up as much as possible and that requires establishing your stake early but not before you have completed your investigative work. Filings that do not indicate an initial intended takeover give you more time to do your homework and investment analysis. In addition to investigating the company's underlying financial and operating strengths you want to pay close attention to trading activity in the firm's shares which can tip you off to a takeover move in the making.

In the same vein, followup Schedule 13D filings represent concrete proof of increased interest in a particular company's shares and takeover possibilities. Astute corporate raiders don't often make the mistake of throwing good money after bad.

Knowing who is acquiring a company's shares is important as well. Warren Buffet and others routinely invest in undervalued situations that return impressive returns over the long-term even though the companies may not be takeover targets. On the other hand, the purchase of shares by one company in the same or closely related industry more often than not indicates a potential takeover attempt in the not-too-distant future. Under both scenarios, your goal is to make extraordinary profits investing in the undervalued company but you probably have less time to evaluate the situation in the takeover scenario. It may take several years for the market to recognize and reward an undervalued situation with a higher stock price while a takeover target's shares can surge 20 to 50 percent within days.

Interest in the target company by several firms bodes well for the takeover investor. Heated bidding wars between two or more acquirers or the emergence of a "white knight" to save the target company from an undesirable suitor typically means surging stock prices and impressive investment gains for investors fortunate and savvy enough to have purchased shares of the takeover target.

Take the months and months of maneuvering and bidding between First Bank System, Inc. and Wells Fargo & Company for First Interstate Bancorp during late 1995 and early 1996. Wells Fargo finally won the bidding war but not before driving up First Interstate's stock price to over $147 per share, more than doubling the low of $67 per share the stock traded for in early 1995 and over seven times First Interstate's stock price as recently as 1991. Needless to say, investors in First Interstate shares were handsomely rewarded for their conviction that the bank with its large multistate branch network was a lucrative takeover target. The $11.5 billion takeover promises to deliver some $1 billion in annual cost savings to Wells Fargo as the company trims staff and merges operations and bank branches.

Barron's and other financial publications obtain their merger and takeover activity information from the *SEC News Digest* which provides daily information on Williams Act filings such as Schedule 13D and other reports. Main advantages of the government report are its timeliness and low subscription cost. One drawback is that it is a summary form and does not include detailed information on the nature of the filing. Another drawback is that the *SEC News Digest* is not indexed. The Security and Exchange Commission is located at 450 Fifth Street, N.W., Washington, D.C. 20549. The telephone number for the Filings, Information and Consumer Services Director is 202-272-7210.

For the computer literate, Disclosure, Inc. and other database providers offer SEC documents on CD-ROM. Disclosure, Inc. can be reached at 5161 River Road, Bethesda, Maryland 20186, 301-951-1300. Charles E. Simon & Company publishes a daily database of M & A Filings containing detailed abstracts of every initial and amended merger and acquisition documents released by the SEC. Check with your library to see what computerized information it carries to ease your investigative trail and financial burden.

No matter when you invest in potential takeover candidates, you want to assure yourself that the takeover makes good economic sense which will be rewarded in higher stock prices and significant investment returns. To get you started in the right direction, the following pages present an analysis of industries undergoing consolidation. Going one step further, potential takeover candidates and acquirers are evaluated for unique investment opportunities designed to allow you to make megabucks on mergers.

Industry and Stock Analysis

Banking and Financial Services

As indicated earlier, the United States banking industry is experiencing unprecedented consolidation and merger and takeover activity which promises to continue unabated for years and decades to come. The same holds true for the financial services sector including brokerage firms and insurance companies.

Many banks scored record earnings in 1995 but may be hard-pressed to meet those expectations for 1996 and beyond. Lower interest rates coupled with rising technology costs and slower internal growth opportunities for market shares gains will create additional pressure for bank mergers. Prior to 1994, mergers of equals were typically not met enthusiastically by the market. However, the breaking of the Chemical Bank/Chase Manhattan merger story saw the stock prices of both financial institutions rising some 15 percent.

For the industry as a whole, asset quality is good and balance sheets are improving. Overall, fundamental earnings potential remains favorable. Investors are starting to take note of the benefits of well-planned bank mergers assuming the deal does not get too pricey. Mergers and acquisitions appear the best way for banks to bring on board expensive technology, gain market share, achieve efficiencies and acquire geographical and product extensions and niches.

One way to play the bank merger market is to "buy-the-buyer" by searching out quality acquirers that stand to benefit from strategic acquisitions. By concentrating on solid, well-managed banks, the investor should prosper by the rising fortunes of a consistent performer even if no major mergers are accomplished.

Katrina Blecher, a financial services analyst with Gruntal & Company Inc. in New York City, advocates another investment strategy. She recommends looking for potential acquisition candidates with solid underlying fundamentals.

"These bank merger targets should possess a major market share and not have too much outstanding capital. An attractive acquisition candidate should have a poor efficiency ratio, giving the acquirer an opportunity to benefit from improved operations resulting from cutting overhead and slashing expenses," says Blecher.

Fred A. Cummings, a bank analyst with McDonald & Company Securities, Inc. in Cleveland, Ohio sees the large super-regional banks the likes of BankAmerica Corporation, First Union Corporation and KeyCorp as active acquirers as they move to fill out and expand their regional franchises.

"In today's banking environment, any bank under $40 billion in assets is a potential takeover target," says Cummings.

In addition to investing in banks as potential takeover targets, there's another tack to take. Banks are repurchasing their own shares in record breaking numbers. See Part 2 for a discussion of stock buyback programs and their implications for the investor.

Another way to invest in the rising fortunes of the banking industry is to invest in companies which serve the back office and financial service needs of financial institutions. Companies such as FiServ Inc. and First Data Corporation prosper by fulfilling the data processing and credit card transaction requirements of banks.

Other financial services companies that merit review as attractive acquirers and/or takeover possibilities include insurance firms and mortgage providers. Use the following analysis as a starting point to begin your own merger investigations and investments for superior investment returns.

AmSouth Bancorporation

P.O. Box 11007
Birmingham, AL 25288
205-320-7151
NYSE: ASO
S & P Rating: B+

Company Profile. AmSouth Bancorporation ranks as the largest bank holding company in Alabama with a territory extending into Florida, Georgia and Tennessee. Over 270 offices serve customer banking needs. The company has been on the acquisition path, building up its Florida operations into the fifth largest in that state. Other forays into nearby Georgia and Tennessee have given AmSouth a toehold in those markets.

Financial Statistics
($ millions except per share and ratio data)

	1993	1994	1995
Assets	13470	16778	17739
Net income (loss)	147	127	175
Long-term debt	173	386	375
Per share data	1993	1994	1995
Earnings (loss)/share	2.89	2.25	3.00
Dividends/share	1.22	1.43	1.52
Selected ratios	1993	1994	1995
Return on average assets	1.19%	0.83%	1.03%
Return on average equity	14.23%	10.24%	12.89%
Stock price range/share	1993	1994	1995
High	35 7/8	34 7/8	41 3/8
Low	27 5/8	25 3/8	25 7/8

Company Strengths. AmSouth enjoys a major market share in Alabama and is making successful inroads into the lucrative bank market of Florida.

A renewed thrust in cost cutting and expanding marketing efforts have started to payoff in improved earnings during the second half of 1995. The company's loan portfolio is well-diversified and with relatively minimal net loan charge-offs.

Investment Assessment. AmSouth's investment potential stems from its attraction to larger financial institutions. The company has delivered uneven earnings per share performance. The bank has reduced expenses, closed branches and moved to beef up marketing efforts but there is still room for improvement. AmSouth's large and growing territory could make it a target for larger Southeast financial institutions desiring to further expand their franchise.

BANK OF BOSTON

100 Federal Street
Boston, MA 02110
617-434-2200
NYSE: BKB
S & P Rating: B-

Company Profile. Bank of Boston has been on the acquisition trail with the purchase of Boston Bancorp and BayBanks, Inc., both announced in late 1995. Bank of Boston's international operations delivered solid profits in 1994 but were hampered in 1995 by Latin American operations in the wake of the Mexico financial crisis. The bank ranks in the top 20 largest bank holding companies in the nation.

Financial Statistics
($ millions except per share and ratio data)

	1993	1994	1995
Assets	40588	44630	46500
Net income (loss)	275	442	545
Long-term debt	1973	2169	2000

Per share data	1993	1994	1995
Earnings (loss)/share	2.28	3.79	4.55
Dividends/share	.40	.93	1.28

Selected ratios	1993	1994	1995
Percent earned net worth	9.4	14.1	14.4
Percent earned total assets	.68	.99	1.15

Stock price range/share	1993	1994	1995
High	29 1/8	29 1/4	50 1/8
Low	20 1/4	22 1/8	25 1/2

Company Strengths. BayBanks brings on board leading-edge technology, an extremely strong retail operation and a wide reaching ATM network. Equally important, the acquisition eliminates Bank of Boston's major rival for banking business and reduces its heavy dependence on international business.

Investment Assessment. The $2 billion BayBanks acquisition sets the stage for a first-rate battle for the Boston area banking market between Bank of Boston and Fleet Financial Group which recently agreed to acquire the U.S. commercial banking unit of National Westminster Bank PLC for $3 billion.

With some $57 billion in assets, Bank of Boston could still be an attractive takeover target. While anti-trust issues may keep Fleet Financial from pursuing Bank of Boston, other large superregional banking institutions desiring to enter the New England market may find Bank of Boston enticing.

Even without a takeover on the horizon, Bank of Boston offers investors an attractive picture with rising earnings and hikes in its cash dividend. The acquisition of BayBanks only makes the future appear brighter. Incidentally, shareholders in BayBanks saw the value of their shares rise from a low of $52 per share in 1995 to $99 per share with takeover rumors in the wind.

THE BANK OF NEW YORK COMPANY, INC.

48 Wall Street
New York, NY 10286
212-495-1784
NYSE: BK
S & P Rating: A

Company Profile. The Bank of New York Company, Inc., ranked as the nation's 16th largest bank holding company prior to a flurry of late 1995 mergers and acquisitions. It operates over 380 branches in New York, New Jersey and Connecticut and maintains an overseas presence with over 29 offices abroad. Management has built a strong financial institution based on an attractive retail franchise and growing securities processing business. Bank of New York has one of the lowest cost structures in the U.S. banking industry.

Financial Statistics
($ millions except per share and ratio data)

	1993	1994	1995
Assets	45546	48879	53720
Net income (loss)	559	749	914
Long-term debt	1590	1774	1848
Per share data	1993	1994	1995
Earnings (loss)/share	2.72	3.70	4.30
Dividends/share	.86	1.10	1.36
Selected ratios	1993	1994	1995
Return on average assets	1.20%	1.49%	1.72%
Return on average equity	14.98%	18.49%	19.42%
Stock price range/share	1993	1994	1995
High	31 1/4	32 5/8	48 3/4
Low	25 1/4	25 1/16	29

Company Strengths. Over 25 percent of bank revenues derive from fee-based services such as securities processing. Alexander Hamilton founded the Bank of New York in 1784 and it has achieved 212 consecutive years of dividend payments, the longest string of any New York Stock Exchange company. The bank is a leading lender and arranger of bank loans to the media and telecommunications industries and has the largest affinity card program in the nation. It has delivered consistent growth over the long-term.

Investment Assessment. Bank of New York runs a first class operation with stable earnings growth in both the banking and processing segments of the business. Look for continued earnings per share growth and dividends hikes. While not a major acquirer in the past, Bank of New York will expand its processing business through internal growth and key acquisitions if the price is right.

NATIONSBANK CORPORATION

NationsBank Corporate Center
Charlotte, NC 28255
704-386-5000
NYSE: NB
S & P Rating: A-

Company Profile. NationsBank has been an aggressive acquirer in recent years with the purchase of Intercontinental Bank, thrift CSF Holdings and BankSouth for $1.6 billion in late 1995/early 1996. The bank itself was formed in the 1991 merger of NCNB Corporation and C & S/Sovran Corporation. Over 2,000 branches blanket the Southeastern states and nearby market areas including Florida, Georgia, Maryland, North Carolina, Tennessee, Texas, Virginia and Washington, D.C.

Financial Statistics
($ millions except per share and ratio data)

	1993	1994	1995
Assets	157686	169604	187298
Net income (loss)	1501	1690	1950
Long-term debt	8352	8488	17775
Per share data	1993	1994	1995
Earnings (loss)/share	5.00	6.12	7.13
Dividends/share	1.64	1.88	2.08
Selected ratios	1993	1994	1995
Return on average assets	.97%	1.02%	1.03%
Return on average equity	15.00%	16.10%	17.01%
Stock price range/share	1993	1994	1995
High	58	57 3/8	74 3/4
Low	44 1/2	43 3/8	44 5/8

Company Strengths. First and foremost, NationsBank is an acquirer adept at seeking out value and improving on operations of merged banks. Recent acquisitions give the company a strong position in the booming Florida and Georgia markets. In addition, rising fee-based revenues contribute to stable and growing earnings.

Investment Assessment. NationsBank will continue searching for strategic acquisitions and could be in the position to seek control of Florida's Barnett Banks, Inc. A strong regional economy bolstering loan demand, cost control and rising fee income promise to deliver impressive earnings per share gains. Likewise, rising profits translate into future dividend hikes.

BONUS BANKING CANDIDATES

Bank	Exchange/Symbol	Comment
Barnett Banks, Inc.	NYSE: BBI	Large independent in lucrative Florida market
Boatman's Bancshares	NASDAQ: BOAT	Largest bank holding company in Missouri, major move into Kansas with Fourth Financial Corporation purchase
Fifth Third Bancorp	NASDAQ: FITB	Aggressive acquirer and strong earnings growth
Fleet Financial Group	NYSE: FLT	Largest New England player with Shawmut National Corporation acquisition
Huntington Bancshares	NASDAQ: HBAN	Smaller player in Ohio and related markets
Liberty Bancorp, Inc.	NASDAQ: LBCI	Chicago market thrift with potential to be acquired
Old Kent Financial	NASDAQ: OKEN	Branches in Michigan and Illinois consolidating markets
U.S. Bancorp	NASDAQ: USBC	Largest bank holding company in Northwest, turnaround in progress
Vectra Banking	NASDAQ: VTRA	Takeover candidate in consolidating Colorado market
Victoria Bankshares	NASDAQ: VICT	Texas-based takeover target
West Coast Bancorp	NASDAQ: WCBO	Strong bank and fee income

Zions Bancorporation	NASDAQ: ZION	Lucrative Rocky Mountain franchise, second largest bank in Utah

Mergers and acquisitions have also taken place in the ranks of financial services firms. The following companies represent a cross-section of companies serving the financial industry or operating in specialized financial services segments

AMERICAN INTERNATIONAL GROUP, INC.

70 Pine Street
New York, NY 10270
212-770-6293
NYSE: AIG
S & P Rating: A+

Company Profile. American International Group is a holding company and the nation's largest underwriter of commerical and industrial coverages. AIG also maintains a strong global presence as the leading U.S-based international insurance organization. Approximately one-third of underwriting premiums derive from foreign operations. Other lines of business include life insurance, mortgage guaranty insurance, aviation insurance as well as claims and risk management services.

Financial Statistics
($ millions except per share and ratio data)

	1993	1994	1995
Assets	101015	114346	134136
Revenues	20135	22442	25870
Net income (loss)	1939	2176	2510
Per share data	1993	1994	1995
Earnings (loss)/share	4.07	4.58	5.30
Dividends/share	.26	.29	.32

32

Selected ratios	1993	1994	1995
Combined loss and expense	100.07	98.75	97.04
Percent earned net worth	12.70	13.20	13.10

Stock price range/share	1993	1994	1995
High	66 7/8	67 1/8	95 1/2
Low	48 7/8	54 5/6	64 1/8

Company Strengths. Unlike many insurance companies, American International Group has achieved a long history of steadily increasing earnings per share and rising dividends. The company's global position and financial strength allow it to perform well when the earnings of other industry firms are under pressure. A well-diversified product mix and conservative investment posture are other strengths.

Investment Assessment. An industry leader, American International Group has invested in other industry companies such as its $200 million purchase of the convertible preferred stock of Alexander & Alexander Services, Inc., an important source of business for AIG and one of the nation's leading independent insurance brokerage companies. Look for earnings and dividends to rise significantly as AIG captures more market share from less financially strong and well-run insurance companies.

FEDERAL NATIONAL MORTGAGE ASSOCIATION

See discussion of Federal National Mortgage Association in the writeup of companies repurchasing their stock in Part 2.

FIRST DATA CORPORATION

401 Hackensack Avenue
Hackensack, NJ 07601
201-525-4702
NYSE: FDC
S & P Rating: NR

Company Profile. First Data Corporation became the nation's largest information processing company with completion of the nearly $7 billion acquisition of First Financial Management Corporation in late 1995. The combined company ranks as the world's largest processor of credit-card transactions for banks and merchants. A recent entry into mutual fund account management opens up new markets and income opportunities. Stringent attention to cost control and efficiency gives First Data a competitive edge as the industry low-cost provider of services.

Financial Statistics.
($ millions except per share and ratio data)

	1993	1994	1995
Working capital	19	243	395
Revenues	1490	1652	4081
Net income/loss	173	208	(84)
Long-term debt	521	475	825
Per share data	1993	1994	1995
Earnings (loss)/share	1.56	1.87	(.39)
Dividends/share	.12	.12	.12
Selected ratios	1993	1994	1995
Percent earned net worth	18.1	20.5	—
Net profit margin	11.6	12.6	—
Stock price range/share	1993	1994	1995
High	42 1/4	50 5/8	71 1/4
Low	31 1/4	40 1/2	46

Company Strengths. First Data management runs a superior operation that will only be enhanced by the Financial Management purchase. In addition, the acquisition brings on board significant electronic banking capabilities and the Western Union operation which controls 90 percent of the world market for money-wiring business.

Investment Assessment. With its major competitor out of the way, First Data will move to strengthen its share of the market and expand into related services. Expect First Data to gobble up smaller industry companies in the months and years ahead. Double digit earnings growth in the range of 15 percent to 20 percent will continue unabated. Since going public in 1992 First Data's share price has been on a steady uptrend, climbing from around $21 per share to over $80 per share in the first half of 1996. The 1995 results were impacted by merger related charges of $2.43 per share.

FISERV, INC.

255 Fiserv Drive
Brookfield, WI 53045
414-879-5000
NASDAQ: FISV
S & P Rating: B+

Company Profile. Fiserv, Inc. provides a variety of back office services to banks, thrifts, credit unions and others. Its product line includes data processing services, trust administration and processing services for retirement plans, business forms design and supply and asset/liability management software and services.

Financial Statistics
($ millions except per share and ratio data)

	1993	1994	1995
Working capital	84	88	245
Revenues	468	580	703
Net income (loss)	31	40	(60)
Long-term debt	111	144	381
Per share data	1993	1994	1995
Earnings (loss)/share	.83	.99	(1.36)
Dividends/share	—	—	—

Selected ratios	1993	1994	1995
Percent earned net worth	10.0	10.6	—
Net profit margin	6.7	6.7	—

Stock price range/share	1993	1994	1995
High	23 7/8	23 7/8	31
Low	16 7/8	18	21

Company Strengths. Fiserv, Inc. benefits from the drive by financial institutions to streamline operations and improve efficiency by outsourcing back office and service functions. In addition, Fiserv has long been an active acquirer itself, most recently purchasing privately-held banking software and service provider Information Technology Inc. and Document Management Services.

Investment Assessment. Revenues and earnings growth will be paced by additional acquisitions and internal growth. The introduction of related services will also bolster financial results. All of this adds up to better than 20 percent growth forecast for at least the next half decade. Merger related charges impacted 1995 results by $2.49 per share.

RELIASTAR FINANCIAL CORPORATION

20 Washington Avenue South
Minneapolis, MN 55440
612-372-5432
NYSE: RLR
S & P Rating: B+

Company Profile. I first covered this insurance holding company when it was known as NWNL Companies. ReliaStar markets group life and health insurance as well as group annuity contracts and life/ health reinsurance.

36

Financial Statistics

($ millions except per share and ratio data)

	1993	1994	1995
Assets	9213	10367	15519
Revenues	1490	1571	2080
Net income (loss)	83	108	169
Per share data	1993	1994	1995
Earnings (loss)/share	3.13	3.08	4.10
Dividends/share	.79	.88	.975
Selected ratios	1993	1994	1995
Percent earned net worth	10.3	13.5	11.9
Stock price range/share	1993	1994	1995
High	38 7/8	34 1/2	44 1/2
Low	24 1/4	27	29

Company Strengths. ReliaStar Financial Corporation is poised to benefit from demographics as baby boomers are entering their prime saving and investing years. Likewise, the company's insurance product areas will thrive in conjunction with the aging of the nation's population. The company is bolstered by a strong balance sheet.

Investment Assessment. The recent merger with USLICO Corporation promises excellent future earnings potential. As the industry further consolidates look for ReliaStar to make additional strategic acquisitions. Double-digit earnings gains in the 14 percent to 15 percent range are in store for the near future. Rising dividends will accompany the improved fortunes of the company.

BANK AND FINANCIAL SERVICES MUTUAL FUNDS

For investors prefering the mutual fund route, the following list of mutual funds specializing in bank and financial services stocks may be your ticket to financial independence.

Fund	Telephone	Returns (thru 12-31-95) One-Year	Three-Year Avg.
Century Shares Trust	800-321-1928	35.23	9.00
Fidelity Select Brokerage	800-544-8888	19.89	13.99
Fidelity Select Home Fin.	800-544-8888	48.89	24.85
Fidelity Select Financial	800-544-8888	42.92	17.42
Fidelity Select Reg. Banks	800-544-8888	42.36	16.62
John Hancock Reg. Banks	800-225-5291	46.56	121.08
Invesco Strategic Financial	800-525-8085	39.81	17.89
Paine Webber Reg. Fin. Gr.	800-647-1568	47.69	17.38
SIFE Trust Fund	800-524-7433	42.42	15.32

Health Care

The health care industry includes the biotechnology, health care providers, medical devices, medical supplies, pharmaceutical and retail drug and drug wholesaler market segments; all of which have experienced a great deal of consolidation in recent years.

CARDINAL HEALTH INC.

655 Metro Place South, Suite 925
Dublin, OH 43017
614-761-8700
NYSE: CAH
S & P Rating: A-

Company Profile. Cardinal Health has grown into the nation's third largest distributor of drugs, medical/surgical supplies and health and beauty products to hospitals, managed care facilities and pharmacies through an active acquisition program. Growth is in a healthy trend. Through a combination of increased market penetration and strategic acquisitions, Cardinal Health's revenues have surged at a 66 percent annual rate to reach $8 billion.

Financial Statistics.
($ millions except per share and ratio data)

| | *Fiscal Year Ending June 30* | |
	1994	*1995*
Working capital	471	601
Revenues	5790	7806
Net income (loss)	34	85
Long-term debt	210	209
Per share data	1994	1995
Earnings (loss)/share	.86	2.10
Dividends/share	.10	.12
Selected ratios	1994	1995
Percent earned net worth	17.2	15.5
Net profit margin	1.1	1.1

| *Stock price range/share* | | *Calendar Year* | |
	1993	*1994*	*1995*
High	38 5/8	48 1/4	58 1/8
Low	19 5/8	33 1/8	41 1/2

*1993 not shown because of change in fiscal year end dates

Company Strengths. I first covered Cardinal Health back in 1987 when it was still called Cardinal Distribution. Since then Cardinal Chairman and Chief Executive Officer Robert D. Walter has increased revenues more than sixteen fold to $8 billion. For the ten-year period through fiscal 1995, Cardinal Health has provided investors with an average annual total return of 28.7 percent, the 15th highest of all Fortune 500 companies. While the size of the company has changed dramatically, its basic operating procedures have not. Walter still stresses the company's Cardinal Rule, "Provide the customer with value added product and support services." Cardinal is a master at squeezing out efficiencies through automation and well-located distribution systems. Adding consistency to revenues and earnings, much of Cardinal Health's business is under multi-year contracts in the hundreds of millions of dollars.

Investment Assessment. Cardinal Health is a leader in the industry and will capitalize on the continued shrinking of wholesalers serving health care providers and pharmacies. While adding market share in its existing businesses and market segments, Cardinal also adds to the bottom line with related acquisitions. For example, the $348 million acquisition of Medicine Shoppe International in 1995 brings into the company a pharmacy franchise operation with nearly 1,000 stores nationwide. The 1996 $870 million acquisition of Pyxis Corporation moves Cardinal closer to becoming a "marketing partner" with major drug manufacturers. Gross margins promise to improve as Cardinal shifts its operations to more high-end, value added services. Street estimates place fiscal 1997 earnings at $3.00 per share, a 50 percent increase over fiscal 1995. Cardinal has split its stock four times since 1989. See the discussion of stock splits and their meaning to investors in Part 2.

COLUMBIA/HCA HEALTHCARE CORPORATION

One Park Plaza
Nashville, TN 37203
615-327-9551
NYSE: COL
S & P Rating: NR

Company Profile. Columbia/HCA Healthcare Corporation is the nation's largest healthcare service company and getting larger with key acquisitions. The $3.3 billion purchase of HealthTrust Inc. created the largest hospital merger in U.S. history and removed Columbia/HCA's largest competitor.

Financial Statistics
($ millions except per share and ratio data)

	1993 *	*1994* *	*1995*
Working capital	573	783	1462
Revenues	10252	11132	17695
Net income/loss	673	850	1299
Long-term debt	3335	3853	7137
Per share data	1993	1994	1995
Earnings (loss)/share	1.98	2.40	2.90
Dividends/share	.26	.12	.12
Selected ratios	1993	1994	1995
Percent earned net worth	19.4	16.9	19.6
Net profit margin	6.6	7.6	7.3
Stock price range/share			
	1993	1994	1995
High	33 7/8	45 1/4	54
Low	10 7/8	33 1/4	35 3/8

* not restated for poolings.

Company Strengths. Columbia/HCA HealthCare Corporation is benefitting from industry wide cost containment pressures and the trend toward managed care. The company's same-facility admissions are outpacing the rest of the industry with an increase of 3 percent for 1995. Strong operating margins and healthy cash flows will fuel additional mergers and help Columbia/HCA Healthcare capture more market share in the years ahead.

Investment Assessment. Columbia/HCA Healthcare's broad revenue base with operations in 36 states and 2 foreign countries adds stability to revenues and earnings. Additional acquisitions and joint ventures with regional providers should provide more market inroads. The company's double-digit earnings growth is projected to continue into the next century. The Internal Revenue Service had taken exception to tax calculations of Columbia/HCA Healthcare predecessor companies for prior years. The Tax Court found in Columbia/HCA's favor in a March 1996 ruling.

JOHNSON & JOHNSON

501 George Street
New Brunswick, NJ 08903
908-524-0400
NYSE: JNJ
S & P rating: A+

Company Profile. Johnson & Johnson is the world's largest manufacturer of healthcare products with a worldwide market of more than 175 countries. In mid-November Cordis Corporation ended its resistance to Johnson & Johnson's hostile takeover, agreeing to a $1.8 billion stock swap. The combined company's annual revenues will reach $1 billion, more than twice its nearest competitor. Johnson & Johnson's pharmaceutical business is growing at a nearly 25 percent clip and more than two dozen acquisitions in the past five years have opened up new markets and kept growth in the consumer and professional segments moving ahead.

Financial Statistics
($ millions except per share and ratio data)

	1993	1994	1995
Working capital	2005	2414	2155
Revenues	14138	15734	18842
Net income/loss	1787	2006	2403
Long-term debt	1493	2199	2125
Per share data	1993	1994	1995
Earnings (loss)/share	2.74	3.12	3.72
Dividends/share	1.01	1.13	1.28
Selected ratios	1993	1994	1995
Percent earned net worth	32.1	28.2	28.0
Net profit margin	12.6	12.7	12.8
Stock price range/share	1993	1994	1995
High	50 3/8	56 1/2	92 3/8
Low	35 5/8	36	53 5/8

Company Strengths. Heavy demand for pharmaceuticals and advanced medical devices bodes well for Johnson & Johnson. The acquisition of Cordis, a leader in angiography and angioplasty, is estimated to add $1 per share to earnings in 1996 alone. A large research and development thrust comprising 8 percent of sales fuels new product development. The company's broad line of highly profitable health care and consumer products and worldwide markets makes this stock a recession-resistant choice for defensive investors searching for excellent total return prospects.

Investment Assessment. For investors who missed out on the substantial price rise as a result of the takeover bid, Johnson & Johnson looks like a solid pick going forward. The company's stock price jumped $6 per share with the release of fourth quarter 1995 results which increased 22 percent to 72 cents per share. Earnings per share are estimated to grow to the $4.50 to $4.95 per share range by 1997. Dividends have increased at a better than 14 percent annual rate over the past ten years.

The Merger Fund was one investor which profited handsomely from the Cordis/Johnson & Johnson transaction. When Johnson & Johnson postponed moving forward on the acquisition in January 1996, the price of Cordis' stock plummeted $10 per share. The Merger Fund used that opportunity to increase its position in Cordis and compound its investment gain.

MERCK & COMPANY

See the analysis of Merck & Company in the discussion of stock repurchase programs and their meaning to investors in Part 2.

PFIZER, INC.

235 East 42nd Street
New York, NY 10017-5755
212-573-2323
NYSE: PFE
S & P rating: A-

Company Profile. Pfizer, Inc. is a global health care company providing products in four major markets segments: animal health, consumer health care, food science and health care. Management's heavy emphasis on research and development keeps the company's product pipeline full. The acquisition of Animal Health made Pfizer the world leader in veterinary products. International operations generate nearly 50 percent of revenues and one-third of operating profits.

Financial Statistics
($ millions except per share and ratio data)

	1993	*1994*	*1995*
Working capital	1290	963	965
Revenues	7162	7977	10021
Net income/loss	658	1298	1573
Long-term debt	571	604	833
Per share data	1993	1994	1995
Earnings (loss)/share	1.03	2.09	2.50
Dividends/share	.84	.94	1.04
Selected ratios	1993	1994	1995
Percent earned net worth	30.5*	30.0	33.0
Net profit margin	15.8	15.7	15.1
Stock price range/share	1993	1994	1995
High	37 7/8	39 3/4	66 7/8
Low	26 1/4	26 5/8	37 1/4

* not including restructuring changes

Company Strengths. As mentioned, Pfizer's research and development program is a strong plus for future growth. In addition, key acquisitions have brought new products and markets into the fold. A number of potentially significant new products are in final testing and approval stages. Pfizer's financial strength and solid cash flow will keep the company in the forefront of industry leaders.

Investment Assessment. Aggressive cost cutting coupled with surging revenues from new products spell a healthy bottom line for Pfizer for the foreseeable future. Earnings are projected to improve over 17 percent to $2.90 per share in 1996 and $3.25 per share in 1997. Dividends are increasing at a double digit clip making Pfizer a solid total return choice with significant growth prospects.

BONUS HEALTH CARE CANDIDATES

Company	Exchange/Symbol	Comment
Becton Dickinson	NYSE: BDX	Record earnings, strong finances, global market, potential merger candidate
Biogen, Inc.	NASDAQ: BGEN	Takeover rumors have set off stock price volatility
Boston Scientific	NYSE: BSX	Strategic acquisitions position BSX in minimally invasive surgical devices market, revenues and earnings on solid uptrend
Healthsouth Corp.	NYSE: HRC	Surgical Care acquisition bolsters network of outpatient surgery centers and bottom line.
N. Amer. Biologicals	NASDAQ: NBIO	Univax merger expands blood products market
OrthoLogic	NASDAQ: OLGC	Strong sales growth, nearing profitability, orthopaedic trauma products niche
Penederm Inc.	NASDAQ: DERM	Partnership marketing for its dermatology drugs could lead to merger or takeover

St. Jude Medical	NASDAQ: STJM	Major cardiac and other acquisitions propelling earnings upward.
United Healthcare	NYSE: UNH	Aggressive acquisitions make UNH one of largest managed-care providers.

For investors prefering the mutual fund route, the following health care mutual funds provide food for thought and can be an excellent source of individual companies to investigate for possible investment.

HEALTH CARE MUTUAL FUNDS

		Returns (thru 12-31-95)	
Fund	Telephone	One-Year	Three-Year Avg.
Dean Witter Health Sciences	800-869-3863	62.30%	17.03%
Fidelity Select Biotech	800-544-8888	44.63	6.02
Fidelity Select Health Care	800-544-8888	41.49	20.74
Fidelity Select Med Del	800-544-8888	28.22	17.48
Franklin Strategic Gl Heal	800-632-2301	57.69*	24.38*
G.T Global Health Care A	800-548-9994	36.96	12.12
Invesco Strategic Health	800-525-8085	58.89	16.92
Medical Research Investment	800-262-6631	61.58	27.34
Putnam Health Sciences Tr A	800-225-1581	47.00	NA
Vanguard Specialized Health	800-662-7447	45.17	24.63

* For the periods ended January 31, 1996

Industrial

In efforts to remain globally competitive, industrial firms are forging mergers and acquisitions at an unprecedented pace. Likewise, companies with lucrative cash hoards and healthy cash flows attract takeover artists such as Chrysler Corporation's huge cash treasure trove invited Kirk Kerkorian to make a mega-bid for the automotive giant. While Kerkorian's raid attempt ended up in a five-year standstill agreement, the market's reaction to the takeover move pushed Chrysler's stock price above $59 per share from a 1995 low of $38 1/4 per share before the Kerkorian threat.

There is plenty more merger and acquisition action coming in the months ahead. The following industrial companies represent an excellent place to begin your search for top performers.

BELDEN INC.

7701 Forsyth Boulevard, Suite 800
St. Louis, MO 63105
314-854-8000
NYSE: BWC
S & P Rating: NR

Company Profile. Belden, Inc. is a leading designer and manufacturer of wire cable and cord products serving international computer, audio/video, industrial and electrical markets. The company has a reputation for quality products. Foreign sales are increasing dramatically and now account for nearly 20 percent of total revenues.

Financial Statistics
($ millions except per share and ratio data)

	1993	1994	1995
Working capital	61	64	90
Revenues	384	440	609
Net income (loss)	32	38	46
Long-term debt	68	37	81
Per share data	1993	1994	1995
Earnings (loss)/share	1.21	1.46	1.76
Dividends/share	—	.20	.20

Selected ratios	1993	1994	1995
Operating margin	14.3	14.9	13.1
Net income/revenues	8.2	8.7	7.6

Stock price range/share	1993	1994	1995
High	18 5/8	22 1/2	29 7/8
Low	14 1/4	16 1/8	19 3/4

Company Strengths. Belden, Inc. is a leader in the design and development of wire and cable products to serve customer specific requirements. An efficient distribution channel gets its products to markets near and far. As a major player in the fragmented specialty wire and cable business, Belden is well positioned to capitalize on acquisition opportunities as they arise.

Investment Assessment. Expanding international market penetration coupled with innovative new product introductions will keep Belden's earnings per share growing at a record double digit clip for the foreseeable future. A well-performing 1993 spin-off from Cooper Industries, Inc., Belden could become a takeover target itself. In the meantime, rising earnings should spur additional stock price gains.

CRANE COMPANY

100 First Stamford Place
Stamford, CT 06902
203-363-7300
NYSE: CR
S & P Rating: B+

Company Profile. Crane Company's history stretches back to 1855. The company is a diversified manufacturer of engineered industrial products serving the aerospace, construction, defense and other industries. It makes everything from aircraft brake systems to vending machines and from control valves to plumbing fixtures.

Crane has been an active domestic acquirer through the years but more recently accelerated picking up foreign operations such as the Kessel PTE, Ltd. plastic-lined pipe manufacturer with facilities in Singapore, Malaysia and Thailand.

In 1994, Crane recognized the substantial undervaluation of Mark Controls, then trading around $8 per share. It eventually acquired Mark Controls with a bid of $17.50 per share and absorbed it into the global Crane Valves operations. The addition of Mark Controls helped that business segment boost operating earnings by over 150 percent in 1995.

Financial Statistics
($ millions except per share and ratio data)

	1993	1994	1995
Working capital	122	236	257
Revenues	1310	1653	1782
Net income (loss)	49	56	76
Long-term debt	106	331	281
Per share data	1993	1994	1995
Earnings (loss)/share	1.62	1.86	2.50
Dividends/share	.75	.75	.75
Selected ratios	1993	1994	1995
Percent earned net worth	16.8	17.1	20.3
Net profit margin	3.7	3.4	4.3
Stock price range/share	1993	1994	1995
High	30 7/8	29 1/2	39 1/2
Low	22 5/8	24 1/8	25 7/8

Company Strengths. Crane Company combines strong internal growth with key acquisitions to deliver impressive earnings gains. A broadly diversified customer base and rising foreign revenues help reduce regional economic risk. A higher backlog entering 1996 works well for continued upward progress on the revenues and earnings front.

Investment Assessment. Higher working capital and rising cash flow put Crane in line to make acquisitions geared to deliver added market share and higher earnings. Look for earnings to rise 20 percent to $3.00 per share in 1996.

DURIRON COMPANY

3100 Research Boulevard
Dayton, OH 45420
513-476-6100
NASDAQ: DURI
S & P Rating: B+

Company Profile. Duriron Company manufacturers corrision-resistant equipment for the chemical processing industries. Major product lines include pipes, pumps and valves. The company serves a global market and has been active on the acquisition trail domestically with the 1995 purchase of Durametallic Corporation for $150 million in stock and overseas with the purchases of Sereg Vannes S.A. in 1994 and Mecair, s.p.a. in 1993.

Financial Statistics*
($ millions except per share and ratio data)

	1993	1994	1995
Working capital	94	114	135
Revenues	314	461	533
Net income (loss)	16	24	31
Long-term debt	35	43	52
Per share data	1993	1994	1995
Earnings (loss)/share	.84	.99	1.42
Dividends/share	.40	.42	.46
Selected ratios	1993	1994	1995
Return on average net assets	8.9%	9.1%	13.0%
Return on average equity	13.1%	12.9%	19.0%

50

Stock price range/share	1993	1994	1995
High	18 1/4	20	30 1/4
Low	13 3/4	14 3/8	17

* 1994 and 1995 figures adjusted for Durametallic merger

Company Strengths. A number of successful acquisitions are driving both revenues and earnings as Duriron penetrates new markets and achieves economies of scale from its combined operations. Strong financials will allow the company to make key acquisitions in the future. A broad customer base from food processing to petrochemicals provides a recession-resistant revenue base.

Investment Assessment. The Durametallic acquisition will spur revenues and earnings in 1996 and beyond. Management will continue to ferret out unique opportunities to enhance earnings via expansion into new markets and product lines as the result of acquisitions.

EMERSON ELECTRIC COMPANY

8000 West Florissant Avenue St. Louis, MO 63163
314-553-2000
NYSE: EMR
S & P Rating: A+

Company Profile. Emerson Electric Company has achieved a long string of record earnings built on a solid foundation of successful acquisitions and internal growth. The company manufactures a wide range of electrical and electronic products and process control systems which it markets on a global basis. Its operations are well-balanced with commercial and industrial segments generating 57 percent of revenues with the rest coming from the appliance and construction product lines.

Financial Statistics.
($ millions except per share and ratio data)

	Fiscal Years Ending September 30		
	1993	*1994*	*1995*
Working capital	382	721	503
Revenues	8174	8607	10012
Net income (loss)	708	789	908
Long-term debt	438	280	209
Per Share data	1993	1994	1995
Earnings (loss)/share	3.15	3.52	4.06
Dividends/share	1.44	1.56	1.78
Selected ratios	1993	1994	1995
Return on average equity	18.5%	19.1%	19.9%
Stock price range/share	1993	1994	1995
High	62 3/8	65 7/8	81 3/4
Low	52 7/8	56 1/4	61 1/2

Company Strengths. A strong and growing overseas presence boosts overall revenues and earnings. Emerson's management runs a lean ship adding to expanding gross margins. Research and development expenses totaling 4 percent of revenues keep new and improved products flowing to customers.

Investment Assessment. Look for Emerson Electric to continue its winning ways. Even without any new acquisitions, earnings are projected to rise more than 10 percent to $4.50 per share in 1996. Dividends are also increasing at a double digit clip. Emerson is a solid total return candidate.

PRAXAIR, INC.

39 Old Ridgebury Road
Danbury, CT 06810-5113
203-837-2000
NYSE: PX
S & P Rating: NR

Company Profile. Praxair, Inc. ranks as the Western Hemisphere's largest producer of industrial gases and the third largest worldwide. The December 1995 $1.5 billion takeover of CBI Industries brings to the firm existing markets in every South American country. Since its spin-off from Union Carbide in 1992, Praxair has more than doubled earnings per share.

Financial Statistics
($ millions except per share and ratio data)

	1993	*1994*	*1995*
Working Capital	(140)	(49)	(99)
Revenues	2438	2711	3146
Net income (loss)	118	203	262
Long-term debt	964	893	933
Per share data	1993	1994	1995
Earnings (loss)/share	.87	1.45	1.82
Dividends/share	.25	.28	.32
Selected ratios	1993	1994	1995
Return on average equity	25.0%	27.6%	23.3%
Debt-to-capital	58.1%	51.1%	46.0%
Stock price range/share	1993	1994	1995
High	18 5/8	24 1/2	34 1/8
Low	14 1/8	16 1/4	19 3/4

53

Company Strengths. Out from under the restraints of Union Carbide, Praxair is busy expanding revenues and margins both through internal growth and acquisitions. The CBI Industries Inc. takeover puts Praxair in the industrial gases big leagues with over $5 billion in combined revenues. The move positions Praxair to benefit from the trend by U.S. soda companies such as Coca-Cola and PepsiCo to move aggressively into emerging markets.

Investment Assessment. Merging of the two companies' operations will produce significant operating savings plus substantially reduce overhead. More importantly, Praxair gains immediate access to growing markets. The result will be higher earnings per share and additional fuel for stock price gains.

UNITED STATES FILTER CORPORATION

73-710 Fred Waring Drive, Suite 222
Palm Desert, CA 92260
619-340-0098
NYSE: USF
S & P Rating: B-

Company Profile. United States Filter Corporation leads the world in the manufacture of engineered systems for water purification, wastewater treatment, filtration and special separations. Its products serve a variety of purposes worldwide. The company also builds and operates wastewater treatment facilites in the United States and elsewhere.

Financial Statistics
($ millions except per share and ratio data)

| | Fiscal Years Ended March 31 | | |
	1993	1994	1995
Working Capital	22	66	57
Revenues	128	180	272
Net income (loss)	—	(3)	8
Long-term debt	5	63	114

54

Per share data	1993	1994	1995
Earnings (loss)/share	(.12)	(.26)	.51
Dividends/share	—	—	—

Selected ratios	1993	1994	1995
Gross profit	26.9	26.4	28.9
Foreign revenues	18.8	20.5	38.2

Stock price range/share	1993	1994	1995
High	19 1/8	16 1/8	27
Low	11 1/8	12 1/8	14 7/8

Company Strengths. Since going public in 1991 United States Filter Corporation has increased revenues more than tenfold to over $440 million in 1996. Internal expansion contributes around 15 percent with the balance attributed to key acquisitions. The company's wide array of products and services forms a solid base for picking up outsourcing operations.

Investment Assessment. An improved sales mix, greater efficiencies and greater market share through acquisitions point to good prospects for United States Filter's bottom line. Continued earnings enhancement promises to deliver higher stock prices in the years ahead.

Natural Resources

Natural resource companies are undergoing a variety of changes from mergers and acquisitions to spin-offs which will be covered in Part 2. The following analysis not only includes traditional natural resource companies such as mining and forest products firms but also incorporates an analysis of corporations operated in related industry segments such as oilfield services and paper products.

BAKER HUGHES INC.

3900 Essex Lane
P.O. Box 4740
Houston, TX 77210-4720
713-439-8600
NYSE: BHI
S & P Rating: B

Company Profile. A product of the 1987 merger of Baker International Corporation and Hughes Tool Company, Baker Hughes Inc. is a direct beneficiary of the consolidating oilfield services industry. The oil bust in the 1980s sank many companies and required the merger of others for survival. The restructuerd Baker Hughes operation is gaining market share and is well-positioned to post significantly higher profits on increased revenues in the years ahead as oil drilling efforts increase.

Financial Statistics
($ millions except per share and ratio data)

	Fiscal Years Ended September 30		
	1993	*1994*	*1995*
Working Capital	921	855	985
Revenues	2702	2505	2637
Net income/loss	59	43	105
Long-term debt	936	638	798
Per share data	1993	1994	1995
Earnings (loss)/share	.34	.22	.57
Dividends/share	.46	.46	.46
Selected ratios	1993	1994	1995
Percent earned net worth	6.2	5.6	6.2
Net profit margin	3.7	3.6	4.0
Stock price range/share	1993	1994	1995
High	29 5/8	22 1/8	24 7/8
Low	18 1/2	17	16 3/4

Company Strengths. Baker Hughes Inc.'s worldwide expertise in oilfield products and services stands the company in good stead to gain market share. More than 40 percent of annual revenues derive from foreign operations. Additional outsourcing by major oil companies is a big plus for Baker Hughes. Likewise, its leadership position in oilfield technology translates into additional business. Finally, a strong market presence keeps Baker Hughes operations humming. For example, despite a 2.4 percent decline in worldwide rig activity in fiscal 1995 ended September 30, 1995 Baker Hughes operating earnings increased more than 40 percent.

Investment Assessment. Moving into fiscal 1996, Baker Hughes' first quarter earnings surged more than 50 percent to 23 cents per share versus 15 cents per share for fiscal 1995's first three months. Results were strong worldwide with Europe, the Gulf of Mexico and Latin America operations driving revenue and earnings gains. The stock market is starting to take notice. After languishing in a trading range between $17 per share and $24 per share for most of 1994 and 1995, Baker Hughes' stock price broke through an important resistance point to shoot above $24 per share in early 1996, reaching a 52-week high of $32 7/8 per share before consolidating a bit. Look for Baker Hughes to garner more market share and improve earnings in the process.

CONSOLIDATED PAPERS, INC.

P.O. Box 8050
Wisconsin Rapids, WI 54495-8050
715-422-3111
NYSE: CDP
S & P Rating: B+

Company Profile. Consolidated Papers, Inc. is a leading producer of enamel or "coated" papers serving the printed communications industry. The company gains market share through internal growth and key acquisitions such as the $215 million acquisition of Niagara of Wisconsin Paper Corporation from Pentair Inc. The acquisition will add 242,000 tons of coated paper capacity. Other Consolidated paper products include corrugated containers, lightweight coated packaging papers and paperboard.

Financial Statistics
($ millions except per share and ratio data)

	1993	1994	1995
Working Capital	36	42	74
Revenues	947	1028	1579
Net income/loss	64	87	229
Long-term debt	121	68	197
Per share data	1993	1994	1995
Earnings (loss)/share	1.46	1.97	5.16
Dividends/share	1.28	1.28	1.43
Selected ratios	1993	1994	1995
Percent earned net worth	7.2	8.5	20.0
Net profit margin	7.2	8.1	14.2
Stock price range/share	1993	1994	1995
High	54 1/4	52 3/8	65 3/8
Low	37 1/2	36 1/4	44 7/8

Company Strengths. Consolidated Paper's large share of the coated paper (used for newspaper advertising inserts, brochures and corporate annual reports) market keeps revenues and earnings on the rise despite a slowdown in the overall paper market. The Niagara of Wisconsin Paper acquisition added some $360 million to annual revenues. Increasing its ability to produce lightweight coated specialty papers, Consolidated approved a $166 million expansion scheduled for completion in April 1997 at its Stevens Point Division, boosting production by 55 percent. Since 1989, the company has invested over $1.1 billion in facility and equipment improvements.

Investment Assessment. Earnings surged more than twofold in 1995 to $5.16 per share versus $1.97 per share in 1994. Operating at near capacity for most of 1995 and able to make price rises stick, Consolidated Paper promises to increase earnings in 1996 another 35 percent to $6.90 per share. After stagnating at $1.28 per share for four years, cash dividends jumped nearly 16 percent in 1995 on the basis of earnings improvement and future prospects.

DOW CHEMICAL COMPANY

2030 Dow Center
Midland, MI 48674
517-636-1000
NYSE: DOW
S & P Rating: B

Company Profile. Worldwide player Dow Chemical Company produces more than 2,500 chemical and plastic products in 130 manufacturing sites located in 30 countries. Dow is the industry's most vertically integrated manufacturer, thereby benefitting most from improved volume and pricing trends. One major caveat is in the works with the potential liability for Dow in relation to ongoing silicone breast-implant litigation. More than likely, insurance coverage will bear the brunt of any settlements or court ordered judgements.

Financial Statistics
($ millions except per share and ratio data)

	1993	1994	1995
Working Capital	2001	2075	4953
Revenues	15052	16742	20200
Net income (loss)	637	931	2071
Long-term debt	5902	5303	4705
Per share data	1993	1994	1995
Earnings (loss)/share	2.33	3.37	7.72
Dividends/share	2.60	2.60	2.80
Selected ratios	1993	1994	1995
Return on equity	7.9	11.3	26.9
Foreign sales	50	52	55
Stock price range/share	1993	1994	1995
High	62	79 1/4	78
Low	49	56 1/2	61 3/8

Company Strengths. Dow has disposed of underperforming business units and operations, trimmed operating expenses and raised the cash dividend payout to an attractive 4 percent at the current stock price. An ongoing share buyback program also works to enhance per share earnings. Dow also owns 74 percent of Destec Energy, Inc., one of the largest nonutility power producers. A huge cash position gives Dow the financial leverage to make acquisitions and invest to gain market share.

Investment Assessment. Investor concern over liability issues and a possible downturn in the cyclical chemicals industry has put a damper on Dow Chemical's stock price which trades around the $85 per share level, pushed through the 1994 high of $79 1/4 per share and resistance level. The company represents a solid total return candidate for investors willing to shoulder the liability risk.

FMC CORPORATION

200 East Randolph Drive
Chicago, IL 60601
312-861-6000
NYSE: FMC
S & P Rating: B

Company Profile. FMC Corporation is a company in transition. It has undergone major restructuring in the past few years and is currently investigating disposing of its 80 percent ownership in FMC Gold. FMC Corporation operates in a wide variety of businesses from chemicals to defense to machinery. Foreign sales account for approximately 23 percent of annual revenues.

Financial Statistics

($ millions except per share and ratio data)

	1993	1994	1995
Working Capital	4	107	250
Revenues	3754	4011	4531
Net income (loss)	164	173	216
Long-term debt	750	901	860
Per share data	1993	1994	1995
Earnings (loss)/share	4.45	4.66	5.63
Dividends/share	—	—	—
Selected ratios	1993	1994	1995
Percent earned net worth	—	41.6	33.5
Net profit margin	4.4	4.3	4.7
Stock price range/share	1993	1994	1995
High	54	65 1/8	80
Low	41 1/2	45 1/2	57 1/8

Company Strengths. Elimination of the precious metals business will allow management to concentrate on its successful core businesses. FMC is alert for attractive acquisitions such as the $313 million purchase of pressure-control equipment manufacturer Moorco International Inc. in 1995. The company is committed to increase shareholder value and not timid in its additions and deletions of operations.

Investment Assessment. Street estimates place 1996 earnings at $7.00 per share, a 24 percent rise over 1995. This could be bettered if the precious metals segment gets disposed of in a timely fashion. Along similar lines, additional acquisitions could bring operating synergies and better bottom line profits in the years ahead. Market recognition of a more focused FMC could help boost the stock price out of its less than $70 per share trading range.

GEORGIA-PACIFIC CORPORATION

133 Peachtree Street, N.E.
Atlanta, GA 30303
404-652-4000
NYSE: GP
S & P Rating: B-

Company Profile. Georgia-Pacific Corporation is one of the world's largest manufacturers and distributors of building products, paper and pulp. The company increased its penetration of alternative building materials with the $350 million acquisition of Montreal-based Domtar Inc.'s gypsum wallboard operations.

Financial Statistics
($ millions except per share and ratio data)

	1993	1994	1995
Working Capital	(418)	(463)	833
Revenues	12330	12738	14292
Net income/loss	(18)	293	1018
Long-term debt	4157	3904	4704
Per share data	1993	1994	1995
Earnings (loss)/share	(.21)	3.28	11.29
Dividends/share	1.60	1.60	2.90
Selected ratios	1993	1994	1995
Percent earned net worth	—	11.2	28.9
Net profit margin	—	2.3	7.1
Stock price range/share	1993	1994	1995
High	75	79	95 3/4
Low	55	56 3/4	65 3/4

Company Strengths. Georgia-Pacific Corporation invested approximately $1.3 billion in capital improvements in 1995. That amount will be cut back

62

to $900 million in 1996 in reaction to declining paper prices. Likewise, the company will hunker down with cost reductions. Further reduction of interest rates could be the impetus to jump start the housing industry.

Investment Assessment. While a cyclical downturn in the paper and building industries may be in the offing, Georgia-Pacific could be a good long-term holding with accumulations of the stock on price pullbacks. The current price of $77 per share yields 2.6 percent and is far below its 52-week high of $95 3/4 per share.

KIMBERLY-CLARK CORPORATION

P.O. Box 619100
Dallas, TX 75261-9100
214-281-1200
NYSE: KMB
S & P Rating: A+

Company Profile. The late December 1995 $9.4 billion merger of Kimberly-Clark Corporation and Scott Paper Company created one of the world's largest tissue manufacturers and the nation's second largest household and personal care products firm. The company operates facilities in 32 countries and markets its products in 150 countries. The combined company will have $12 billion in annual revenues after disposition of some units required by the U.S. Department of Justice to prevent monopoly situations in facial tissue and baby wipes.

Financial Statistics
($ millions except per share and ratio data)

	1993	*1994*	*1995*
Working Capital	(233)	(249)	(55)
Revenues	6973	7364	13789
Net income (loss)	511	535	33
Long-term debt	933	930	1985

Per share data	1993	1994	1995
Earnings (loss)/share	3.18	3.33	.12
Dividends/share	1.70	1.75	1.79

Selected ratios	1993	1994	1995
Percent earned net worth	20.8	20.6	30.2
Net profit margin	7.3	7.3	8.0

Stock price range/share	1993	1994	1995
High	62	60	83
Low	44 5/8	47	47 1/4

Company Strengths. Shortly after completion of the Scott Paper merger, Kimberly-Clark announced it would eliminate as many as 10 percent of the company's jobs and dispose of 12 plants. In the fourth quarter of 1995, the company took a $1.4 billion charge associated with the Scott Paper purchase. The moves are expected to provide annual cost savings in excess of $500 million by 1998.

Investment Assessment. The stringent cost cutting and scaling back on duplicate operations and people will generate enormous benefits in the years ahead. More importantly, the combined force of Kimberly-Clark and Scott Paper international clout will help achieve greater market penetration. Earnings are projected to jump to $4.95 per share in 1996 after years of being stalled in the low $3.00 per share range. Enthusiasm over the merger benefits may have pushed the stock to lofty heights. Purchase on market pullbacks for long-term appreciation.

Telecommunications/Computers

Telecommunications, high-tech networking and computer companies are rushing to form mergers and joint ventures to prepare themselves for the interactive world of the next millenium. Cellular firms are combining like never before, software companies are gobbling up smaller competitors and computer companies are fighting for market share with more innovative and powerful hardware and programming. It is an exciting world full of unprecedented investment opportunities.

However, caution is advised. The technology sector can rapidly go out of favor as occurred during the last quarter of 1995 when technology stocks plummeted. Mergers can also take a sour turn as happened to the highly touted and equally disappointing $1.4 billion merger of Novell, Inc. and WordPerfect Corporation in March 1994. Corporate culture clashes between the entities and fierce competition from arch-rival Microsoft Corporation sunk the venture. Novell finally admitted its miscalculations and agreed to sell the WordPerfect software line to Corel Corporation in late December 1995. Novell shareholders paid the price as earnings slipped in 1994 and the company's stock price dropped from its March 1994 high of $26 1/4 per share to a low of $13 7/8 per share in late 1995.

The following analysis provides a sampling of telecommunications and high-tech companies worthy of looking at as prospective investment candidates.

ALLTEL CORPORATION

One Allied Drive
Little Rock, AR 72202
501-661-8000
NYSE: AT
S & P Rating: A

Company Profile. ALLTEL Corporation provides cellular, local and long-distance service to customers in 22 states. The company is aggressively growing its cellular business which now generates over 11 percent of annual revenues. Both cellular and traditional telephone operations are performing well.

Financial Statistics
($ millions except per share and ratio data)

	1993	1994	1995
Working Capital	(115)	87	162
Revenues	2342	2962	3110
Net income (loss)	243	304	355
Long-term debt	1596	1846	1762

65

Per share data	1993	1994	1995
Earnings (loss)/share	1.39	1.43	1.86
Dividends/share	.80	.88	.96

Selected ratios	1993	1994	1995
Percent earned net worth	15.6	18.7	17.4
Net profit margin	10.4	10.3	10.8

Stock price range/share	1993	1994	1995
High	31 1/4	31 3/8	31 1/8
Low	22 7/8	22 7/8	23 1/4

Company Strengths. Strong gains in the cellular business combined with good performance in ALLTEL's core telephone operations serves to raise earnings. Strong finances bolster the rising dividend and provide funds for cellular acquisitions.

Investment Assessment. A solid total return candidate, ALLTEL has increased the common dividend for 35 consecutive years. The company has provided an impressive total annual return in excess of 24 percent for the last ten years. A quality holding for conservative investors.

BAY NETWORKS, INC.

4401 Great America Parkway
Santa Clara, CA 95054
408-988-2400
NYSE: BAY
S & P Rating: NR

Company Profile. Bay Networks, Inc. develops and manufactures a broad line of communications networking products including high-speed routers, wide area network access devices, network switches and network management software. The company took over a major competitor's key supplier with the acquisition of Xylogics Inc. for $300 million in 1995.

Financial Statistics
($ millions except per share and ratio data)

| | Fiscal Years Ended June 30 | | |
	1993	1994	1995
Working capital	464	565	676
Revenues	885	1086	1342
Net income (loss)	101	121	179
Long-term debt	110	110	110
Per share data	1993	1994	1995
Earnings (loss)/share	.59	.71	1.00
Dividends/share	—	—	—
Selected ratios	1993	1994	1995
Percent earned net worth	23.1	21.6	24.0
Net profit margin	11.4	11.1	13.3
Stock price range/share	1993	1994	1995
High	—	20 7/8	49 7/8
Low	—	12 3/8	18 3/8

Company Strengths. Gross margins are on the upswing and will be aided further by the Xylogics acquisition. The move provides Bay Networks direct control of remote access technolgy and products and a competitive edge over some industry companies. A broad product line and increasing market share bode well for the future.

Investment Assessment. Bay Networks' earnings are projected to rise 50 percent in fiscal 1996. The company's stock price has soared since going public in late 1994. From a low of $12 3/8 per share in 1994, Bay Networks peaked at a high of $49 7/8 in late 1995 before settling back to $33 3/8 per share in the first half of 1996. While the company's trading history is short, strong earnings increases should propel the stock to new heights.

FRONTIER CORPORATION

180 S. Clinton Avenue
Rochester, NY 14646
716-777-1000
NYSE: FRO
S & P Rating: B+

Company Profile. Frontier Corporation is a leading telecommunications company and active in adding market share. In 1995, the company acquired 4 long-distance resellers for $430 million and effected a $2 billion merger with ALC Communications, giving the company a national presence.

Financial Statistics
($ millions except per share and ratio data)

	1993	1994	1995
Working capital	11	368	19
Revenues	1437	1608	2144
Net income (loss)	121	180	22
Long-term debt	582	662	619
Per share data	1993	1994	1995
Earnings (loss)/share	.78	1.12	.13
Dividends/share	.80	.82	.84
Selected ratios	1993	1994	1995
Debt ratio	44.6	41.2	41.0
Return on equity*	19.4	21.9	24.0
Stock price range/share	1993	1994	1995
High	25	25 1/4	30
Low	17 1/4	20 1/4	19 1/4

* Before nonrecurring charges

Company Strengths. Frontier Corporation has proven itself an effective competitor on a national scale. The ALC Communications merger makes the company the fifth largest long-distance telephone firm in the nation. As a result, revenues are surging. Now cost containment measures and productivity efficiencies will take precedence as the companies are integrated.

Investments Assessment. Acquisition related costs resulted in a $195 million charge in the third quarter of 1995. Overall, efficiencies and consolidation of operations are expected to save the company around $2 million in benefit costs annually beginning in 1996. Frontier is well-positioned to capture market share and improve earnings performance in the coming years.

MEASUREX CORPORATION

One Results Way
Cupertino, CA 95014-5991
408-255-1500
NYSE: MX
S & P Rating B-

Company Profile. Measurex Corporation is a leading supplier of computer-integrated measurement, control and informations systems and services for continuous and batch manufacturing processes. As companies seek to improve their production operations they turn to Measurex for solutions. The company serves the metals, nonwoven, pulp and paper, rubber and other industrial sectors. Measurex markets to customers in 30 countries around the world. Foreign operations account for 57 percent of annual revenues.

Financial Statistics
($ millions except per share and ratio data)

	1993	1994	1995
Working capital	138	124	89
Revenues	254	260	335
Net income/loss	8	6	27
Long-term debt	17	12	15

Per share data	1993	1994	1995
Earnings (loss)/share	.46	.34	1.60
Dividends/share	.44	.44	.44

Selected ratios	1993	1994	1995
Percent earned net worth	3.9	4.4	16.2
Net profit margin	3.2	3.7	8.0

Stock price range/share	1993	1994	1995
High	21	23 5/8	36
Low	15 7/8	17 1/4	22 1/8

Company Strengths. Measurex is moving away from its heavy dependence on the pulp and paper industry which now accounts for approximately 80 percent of sales. In addition, the company has stressed cost reduction and manufacturing efficiency measures in its own operations. The recent acquisition of Data Measurement gives Measurex an important foothold in the steel industry.

Investment Assessment. Measurex's revenues and earnings surged on the plant expansion explosion in the pulp and paper industry over the past few years. Its stock price more than doubled from its low of $17 1/4 per share in 1994 to $36 per share in 1995. Since then the stock price retreated to the $29 per share level. While the slowdown in the pulp and paper industry will impact results short-term, diversification efforts will keep earnings growing. A solid long-term investment with good price rebound potential.

PARK ELECTROCHEMICAL CORPORATION

5 Dakota Drive
Lake Success, NY 11042
516-354-4100
NYSE: PKE
S & P Rating:

Company Profile. Park Electrochemical Corporation designs and manufactures materials for multilayer printed circuit boards and high performance laminates for electronic original equipment manufacturers. Insiders own approximately 14 percent of outstanding shares. The company operates eight manufacturing facilities including three in Europe and one in Southeast Asia. Foreign operations generate 23 percent of annual revenues.

Financial Statistics
($ millions except per share and ratio data)

| | Fiscal Years ended February 27 | | |
	1993	1994	1995
Working capital	47	46	55
Revenues	175	208	253
Net income (loss)	2	8	17
Long-term debt	34	3	—
Per share data	1993	1994	1995
Earnings (loss)/share	.25	1.01	1.59
Dividends/share	.16	.16	.18
Selected ratios	1993	1994	1995
Percent earned net worth	4.0	13.1	15.5
Net profit margin	1.4	3.9	6.9
Stock price range/share	1993	1994	1995
High	12 1/8	17 7/8	34 1/8
Low	5 7/8	11 3/8	14

Company Strengths. Park Electrochemical Corporation uses a combination of internal research and development efforts and acquisitions to develop advanced technology and high-tech electronic materials to meet customer requirements. Expanded operations and two new production facilities are in the works to meet demand.

Investment Assessment. Following two blockbuster years during which earnings more than doubled, Park continues to run its operations at full capacity. Costs associated with manufacturing capacity expansion will put a slight damper on fiscal 1996 and 1997 earnings but will have a substantial beneficial impact in the following years. Even so, look for fiscal 1996 earnings to climb over 30 percent to $2.10 per share and fiscal 1997 earnings to reach $2.50 per share. The company's broad customer base should keep earnings growing.

BONUS TELECOMMUNICATIONS/ COMPUTER CANDIDATES

Company	Exchange/Symbol	Comment
Cable Design Tech.	NASDAQ: CDTC	A bevy of acquisitions are pacing exploding sales and earnings
Cheyenne Software	AMEX: CYE	Market leader, international position, highly profitable niche market, provides computer backup software and services
Diodes Inc.	AMEX: DIO	Earnings doubled in 1995, key marketing agreement with ITT boosts revenues and market penetration
Hewlett-Packard Co.	NYSE: HWP	Large PC market share and rapidly expanding earnings, earnings per

		share growth over 11 percent annually for past decade, broad customer base with business, engineering and multimedia applications
SunGard Data Systems	NASDAQ: SNDT	Leading company in comprehensive computer disaster recovery systems, steady earnings growth

MISCELLANEOUS MERGER INVESTMENT CANDIDATES

In addition to companies in the industries covered above there's a wealth of investment opportunities in other industries running the gamut from food and beverages to specialized retail and from consumer goods to transportation and utilities. Use the following analysis as a starting point to ferret out your own investment candidates from these and other industry segments.

Company	Exchange/Symbol	Comment
AES Corporation	NASDAQ: AESC	Worldwide independent power producer takes stakes in power generation projects, solid earnings growth
Big B, Inc.	NASDAQ: BIGB	According to Charles Neuhauser, senior vice president with Investment Counselors of Maryland, drug store chain Big B is worth $18 per share on its cash flow characteristics

Campbell Soup Co.	NYSE: CPB	Double digit revenue and earnings gains on combination of internal growth and acquisitions like Salsa maker PaceFoods Ltd.
Carson Pirie Scott	NYSE: CRP	Department store retailer worth $30 per share on its basic business line and another $6-$8 per share based on its credit card operations according to Neuhauser, possible acquisition target
Landstar System Inc.	NASDAQ: LSTR	Niche market in transportation network systems and freight haulers, strong earnings on internal growth and acquisitions
Manpower Inc.	NYSE: MAN	Expanding foreign operations bolster earnings for employee service company
Omnicom Group, Inc.	NYSE: OMC	Worldwide advertising company, uses key acquisitions to penetrate new markets and garner market share
Paychex, Inc.	NASDAQ: PAYX	An active acquisition program expands revenues and earnings for payroll processing giant
The Pep Boys-Manny Moe & Jack	NYSE: PBY	A solid performer in the highly fragmented but consolidating auto parts supply industry

Sherwin-Williams	NYSE: SHW	Major 1995 acquisitions and store upgrades promise to boost earnings in 1996 and beyond
Staples, Inc.	NASDAQ: SPLS	Major office supply superstore chain making acquisitions and joint ventures in Canada and overseas, strong market share gains in fragmented industry
Toro Company	NYSE: TTC	Now that Toro has turned in three successive solid years after a loss in 1992, the company may become an attractive acquisition target
United Stationers	NASDAQ: USTR	Merger gives largest business products wholesaler more market clout
Union Pacific	NYSE: UP	Mergers with Chicago & North Western Corporation and Southern Pacific Rail Corporation strengthen UP's claim to regain ranking as position as the nation's largest rail carrier, the Southern Pacific merger will reap $750 million in annual savings

Global Opportunities

You can also participate in the world of acquisitions, mergers and take-overs on a global scale. Just as American companies shattered mergers and acquisitions records in 1995, the Europeans were hot on their trail. More than $219 billion worth of mergers and acquisitions were recorded in Europe in 1995, shattering the previous record of $158 billion in 1990 at the beginning of the European Union.

Among the larger European deals were the $14.3 billion hostile takeover of Wellcome PLC by arch-rival Glaxco Holdings PLC, the $13 billion combination of Sweden's Pharmacia AB and Upjohn Company and the $7.1 billion acquisition of Marion Merrell Dow Inc. by Germany's Hoechst AG.

Investing in foreign companies through American Depositary Receipts (ADRs) is as easy as investing in American stocks. The ADRs act as a proxy for the foreign shares and are traded on U.S. stock exchanges. Thus ADRs eliminate the complexity of purchasing foreign company shares on foreign stock exchanges. Annual trading in ADRs surpassed $200 billion for the first time in 1993, five times the $40 billion traded in 1988. Today, more than 1,500 ADRs from hundreds of countries are traded on U.S. exchanges.

The following examples represent a number of mergers on an international scale. They include American companies purchasing foreign companies, foreign companies acquiring American firms and one foreign company purchasing another foreign company.

ALUMINUM COMPANY OF AMERICA

425 Sixth Avenue
Pittsburgh, PA 15219
412-553-4545
NYSE: AA
S & P Rating: B-

Company Profile. Aluminum Company of America (Alcoa) ranks as the world's largest producer of aluminum and alumina. It serves customers in the aerospace, automotive, construction, packaging and other industries with a wide variety of fabricated and finished products. Alcoa operates facilities in 26 countries and earns 44 percent of annual revenues from foreign customers. Moving to expand its European presence, Alcoa agreed to acquire Alumix SpA of Italy for $280 million in late 1995.

Financial Statistics
($ millions except per share and ratio data)

	1993	*1994*	*1995*
Working capital	1610	1600	2090
Revenues	9056	9904	12500
Net income (loss)	5	375	791
Long-term debt	1433	1030	1216
Per share data	1993	1994	1995
Earnings (loss)/share	.02	2.10	4.43
Dividends/share	.80	.80	.90
Selected ratios	1993	1994	1995
Return on equity	.1	9.9	18.5
Stock price range/share	1993	1994	1995
High	39 1/4	45 1/8	60 1/4
Low	29 1/2	32 1/8	36 7/8

Company Strengths. As the world's largest aluminum producer Alcoa achieves economies of scale other competitors can not match. Its worldwide position serving a variety of industries also helps offset the effects of a slowdown in any one market sector or regional economy. The company is financially strong and enjoys healthy cash flow.

Investment Assessment. Alcoa is one of the premier companies in the industry. However, it is susceptible to industry cycles. For the near-term look for continued earnings improvement. An ongoing stock buyback program will help boost per share comparisons.

CADBURY SCHWEPPES PLC

25 Berkeley Square
London United Kingdom W1X 6HT

New York Address:
1633 Broadway
New York, NY 10019
212-373-0200
NYSE: CSG
S & P Rating: NR

Company Profile. London-based Cadbury Schweppes PLC manufactures confectionery and beverage products on a worldwide basis. It generates over 50 percent of annual revenues from sales outside of the United Kingdom. Cadbury has been actively seeking acquisitions to expand its market share and get a better foothold in key markets. It also carries on an active licensing program to leverage popular brand names.

Financial Statistics
($ millions except per ADR and ratio data)

	1993	1994	1995 Est.
Working capital	(93)	89	15
Revenues	5513	6326	7700
Net income (loss)	269	348	495
Long-term debt	572	634	1800
Per ADR data	1993	1994	1995
Earnings (loss)/ADR	1.39	1.68	1.90
Dividends/ADR	.98	1.17	1.28
Selected ratios	1993	1994	1995
Percent earned net worth	8.5	9.7	10.0
Net profit margin	4.9	5.5	6.4

Stock price range/ADR	1993	1994	1995
High	31 1/8	32 1/2	35 3/8
Low	25 3/8	25	24 5/8

Company Strengths. Cadbury has been extending its share of the Canadian market with the recent $175 million acquisition of Neilson Cadbury, Canada's largest chocolate bar manufacturer. In the U.S., Cadbury purchased A & W brands in 1993 and Dr. Pepper for $1.7 billion in 1995. Other global forays include the construction of new plants in developing markets such as China, Poland and the former Soviet Union.

Investment Assessment. Cadbury's stock price spiked up in October 1995 on rumors that Unilever Group considered Cadbury an attractive takeover target. You can play this stock based on its success as an acquirer able to deliver consistent earnings increases or as a potential takeover target. Either way, Cadbury is an attractive long-term holding.

CENTRAL & SOUTH WEST CORPORATION

1616 Woodall Rodgers Freeway
Dallas, TX 75266
800-527-5797
NYSE: CSR
S & P Rating: A-

Company Profile. Central & South West Corporation provides electricity to parts of Arkansas, Louisiana, Oklahoma and Texas. The company is determined to expand its presence overseas. After losing out on a bid to acquire Norweb PLC the company came to an agreement to purchase British Seeboard PLC for $2.53 billion in November 1995.

Financial Statistics
($ millions except per share or ratio data)

	1993	1994	1995
Revenues	3687	3623	3730
Net income/loss	344	412	421
Long-term debt	2749	2940	3001
Per share data	1993	1994	1995
Earnings (loss)/share	1.63	2.08	2.10
Dividends/share	1.62	1.70	1.72
Selected ratios	1993	1994	1995
Percent earned net worth	10.5	12.9	13.0
Long-term debt/equity	45.6	46.5	46.0
Stock price range/share	1993	1994	1995
High	34 1/4	30 7/8	28 1/8
Low	28 1/4	20 1/8	22 3/8

Company Strengths. The United Kingdom utility purchase makes good sense in light of its favorable regulatory climate and attractive growth potential. Seeboard has been a successful and innovative utility in its own right and will enhance Central and South West's earnings possibilities and global presence in the electrical and gas-distribution industry segments. The company participates in a number of cogeneration projects in the United States and other countries. It has also formed a new subsidiary, EnerShop, Inc., aimed at helping major energy users reduce their costs.

Investment Assessment. Central and South West Corporation is an interesting long-term play as it moves into the global arena. In the interim, requested rate adjustments spell higher earnings in the years ahead. The stock carries an attractive yield of 6.5 percent.

GLAXCO WELLCOME PLC

Lansdowne House
Berkeley Square
London United Kingdom W1X 6BP

New York Address:
499 Park Avenue
New York, NY 10022
212-308-5186
NYSE: GLX
S & P Rating: NR

Company Profile. Glaxco PLC transformed itself into the world's largest pharmaceutical company with the $14.3 billion acquisition of Wellcome PLC in 1995. Its worldwide operations are paced by the United States generating 43 percent of annual revenues, Europe (22%) and the balance from the rest of the world.

Financial Statistics
($ millions except per ADR and ratio data)

	1993*	1994*	1995 Est.
Working capital	4013	4723	1450
Revenues	7346	8710	15475
Net income (loss)	1709	1933	2120
Long-term debt	316	419	10420
Per ADR data	1993	1994	1995
Earnings (loss)/ADR	1.13	1.27	1.30
Dividends/ADR	.83	1.04	1.19
Selected ratios	1993	1994	1995
Percent earned net worth	24.2	23.7	21.5
Net profit margin	23.2	22.2	13.7
Stock price range/ADR	1993	1994	1995
High	24 1/4	21 5/8	28 3/8
Low	14 7/8	15 7/8	18 3/4

* Calendar years ended June 30.

Company Strengths. Major cost benefits are expected to accrue from the consolidation of the Glaxco/Wellcome operations. These reduced costs will begin to favorably impact earnings in 1998 after the amortization of goodwill and higher interest expenses associated with the Wellcome purchase. On another front, Glaxco Wellcome will raise over $1 billion from the sale of certain drug joint ventures including Sudafed and Neosporin to Warner-Lambert Company. The sales proceeds will be used to par down the debt load taken on with the Wellcome acquisition. Glaxco Wellcome joined forces with other industry companies to invest $2.5 billion in biotech companies during the first half of 1996, a five-fold increase over previous investment levels.

Investment Assessment. Long-term investors will find plenty to like as Glaxco Wellcome's bottom line improves following the merger's positive effects. The sale of nonprescription drug ventures allows management to concentrate its talent and resources on the firm's money-making prescription operations. Consider the 5.2 percent yield a bonus while you wait for higher stock prices.

HONG KONG TELECOMMUNICATIONS LTD.

1 Harbour Road
Hong Kong

New York Address:
777 Third Avenue
New York, NY 10017
212-593-4813
NYSE: HKT
S & P Rating: NR

Company Profile. Hong Kong Telecommunications Ltd. possesses exclusive licenses for international communications services in Hong Kong until 2006. The company has its eye on investment in China with its massive market potential for telecommunications.

Financial Statistics
($ millions except per ADR and ratio data)

	1993	1994	1995 Est.
Revenues	3113	3450	3780
Net income (loss)	930	1099	1200
Long-term debt	—	—	—
Per ADR data	1993	1994	1995
Earnings (loss)/ADR	.83	.99	1.10
Dividends/ADR	.65	.75	.80
Selected ratios	1993	1994	1995
Percent earned net worth	42.6	43.9	45.0
Net profit margin	29.9	31.8	31.8
Stock price range/ADR	1993	1994	1995
High	22 5/8	22 1/8	21 1/2
Low	12	16	16

Company Strengths. Hong Kong Telecommunications Ltd. runs a first-class, efficient operation generating consistent earnings improvement. The company is financially strong with no long-term debt. Over $6 billion in capital investment in 1994 and 1995 bolsters Hong Kong Telecommunications' future growth.

Investment Assessment. Hong Kong Telecommunications Ltd. represents a conservative way to participate in China's economic expansion. Rising earnings and a 4 percent yield make the stock a solid long-term investment.

LUXOTTICA GROUP SpA

Agordo, Belluno 32021 Italy
0039-437-63840
NYSE: LUX
S & P Rating: NR

Company Profile. Luxottica Group SpA of Italy is a global provider of eyeglass frames and sunglasses under well-known brand names such as Brooks Brothers and Giorgio Armani. Luxottica won a bidding war for U.S. Shoe, acquiring the company for $1.3 billion in 1995. Subsequently, as planned, the company sold off the U.S. Shoe women's clothing and footwear businesses but retained the prize jewel LensCrafter operation.

Financial Statistics
($ millions except per ADR and ratio data)

	1993	1994	1995 Est.
Revenues	385	501	1175
Net income (loss)	54	77	95
Long-term debt	8	9	630
Per ADR data	1993	1994	1995
Earnings (loss)/ADR	1.20	1.73	2.15
Dividends/ADR	.42	.49	.48
Selected ratios	1993	1994	1995
Percent earned net worth	26.9	29.1	28.0
Net profit margin	14.0	15.4	8.0
Stock price range/ADR	1993	1994	1995
High	29 7/8	36 5/8	59 3/4
Low	19 5/8	27 5/8	31 1/8

Company Strengths. The LensCrafter unit contributed 34 percent of U.S. Shoe's more than $2 billion in annual revenues and will more than double Luxottica's revenues in 1996 from 1994 levels. Luxottica has built a successful vertically integrated company with expertise in design, manufacture and distribution. The LensCrafter acquisition brings on board an extensive retail network in North America, the world's largest optical market.

Investment Assessment. An excellent long-term investment with promised earnings per share hikes flowing from the LenCrafter purchase. Earnings for 1996 are projected to surpass $2.60 per share, up 50 percent from the 1994's results.

PACIFICORP

700 N.E. Multnomah Street
Portland, OR 97232-4116
503-731-2000
NYSE: PPW
S & P Rating: B+

Company Profile. PacifiCorp expanded its reach far beyond the northwest with the late 1995 $1.6 billion acquisition of Australian utility distribution company Powercor. The move adds 570,000 electric customers to PacifiCorp's 1.3 million customer base.

Financial Statistics
($ millions except per share and ratio data)

	1993	*1994*	*1995*
Revenues	3412	3507	3401
Net income (loss)	423	451	459
Per share data	1993	1994	1995
Earnings (loss)/share	1.40	1.45	1.48
Dividends/share	1.20	1.08	1.08
Selected ratios	1993	1994	1995
Percent earned net worth	11.0	11.1	11.0
Long-term debt/equity	50.5	48.2	47.5

Stock price range/share	1993	1994	1995
High	20 3/4	19 1/2	21 5/8
Low	16 7/8	15 7/8	17 1/2

Company Strengths. In addition to the Australian purchase PacifiCorp is also expanding domestically with negotiations for a Kentucky utility. Earnings are on a solid upward trend after faltering in 1992. The company's financials are also looking stronger with a declining long-term debt ratio.

Investment Assessment. PacifiCorp is a low-cost power provider with an expanding customer base. Higher rates are in the works which will boost 1996 earnings and beyond. Purchase for capital gains and total return underpinned by an attractive yield over 5 percent.

TELE DANMARK

Kannikegarde 16
DK-8000
Aarhus C Denmark
NYSE: TLD
S & P Rating: NR

Company Profile. Tele Danmark is the leading supplier of telecommunications services in Denmark. Currently a good portion of outstanding shares are held by Danish investors. This is likely to change in coming years and enhance investor interest.

Financial Statistics
($ millions except per ADR and ratio data)

	1993	1994	1995
Working capital	345	1678	2380
Revenues	2407	2936	3396
Net income (loss)	231	357	643
Long-term debt	1428	512	466

Per ADR data	1993	1994	1995
Earnings (loss)/ADR	.84	1.36	2.46
Dividends/ADR	—	1.11	1.37
Selected ratios	1993	1994	1995
Percent earned net worth	17.8	7.5	11.3
Net profit margin	9.6	12.1	19.0
Stock price range/ADR	1993	1994	1995
High	—	29 5/8	29 1/4
Low	—	23 1/8	24 1/4

Company Strengths. Tele Danmark is sitting on over $1.2 billion in cash which can be put to good use improving operations, making strategic acquisitions and diversifying. The balance sheet is healthy with relatively little long-term debt.

Investment Assessment. Tele Danmark offers investors an international stake in the telecommunications industry. The more than 5 percent yield is attractive as are projected earnings increases translating into a higher stock price down the road.

UNILEVER N.V.

Weena 455
3013 AL
Rotterdam, The Netherlands

New York Address:
390 Park Avenue
New York, NY 10022
212-906-3398
NYSE: UN
S & P Rating: A

Company Profile. The Unilever Group has two parent holding companies: Unilever N.V. of The Netherlands and Unilever PLC headquartered in Great Britain. The British shares trade as ADRs under the symbol UL while the Dutch shares trade as New York shares under the symbol UN. Unilever is the world's largest producer of brand consumer products.

Financial Statistics
($ millions except per share or ratio data)

	1993	1994	1995 Est.
Working capital	2941	4301	4300
Revenues	41237	47466	54000
Net income (loss)	1787	2293	2635
Long-term debt	2179	3224	3325
Per share data	1993	1994	1995
Earnings (loss)/share	5.98	8.20	9.40
Dividends/share	3.21	3.24	4.00
Selected ratios	1993	1994	1995
Percent earned net worth	13.2	14.6	16.0
Net profit margin	4.3	4.8	4.9
Stock price range/share	1993	1994	1995
High	119 1/8	120 5/8	142 1/8
Low	95 1/2	100 1/8	114 1/4

Company Strengths. Unilever has a stable of universally recognized consumer products under such brand names as Breyer, Lever Brothers, and Lipton. The company is moving to expand its global markets and brand name product base with the purchase of Gorton's seafood operations from General Mills Inc., the purchase of the industrial and institutional cleaning products division of The Molson Companies Ltd for $568 million and the proposed acquisition of Helene Curtis Industries for $770 million.

Investment Assessment. A yield around 3 percent and growth through acquisitions combine to make Unilever an attractive total return portfolio holding for long-term investors. You may opt between the New York based shares or the ADRs of the British unit depending on your anticipation of the direction of foreign currency impacts on company results.

Assessing Merger Candidate Characteristics

Now it's up to you to ferret out attractive investment opportunities to earn significant profits from potential merger candidates or targets. In mergers and takeovers look for firms that can deliver a number of benefits to the acquirer. This can take the form of huge cash reserves; specialized technology; sources of key raw materials; synergies in operation, marketing or key markets; cross-selling opportunities and economies of scale through combined facilities.

On the acquisition side of the coin look for companies with excess cash to invest, firms that can achieve growth faster and cheaper through the purchase of other operations and companies looking to enter new markets either geographically or by product line. Obviously, companies with a track record of successful past mergers and takeovers is a good place to start your search. Also look at fragmented industries in the process of consolidation. In today's economic environment that includes but is not limited to banking, biotechnology, healthcare, insurance, machine tools, natural resources, office supply, retail, transportation and utilities. There are plenty of merger candidates to choose from to earn superior investment earnings. Don't miss out on this once in a lifetime opportunity to participate in the biggest merger boom ever.

PART 2

Turnarounds, Spin-Offs, Stock Splits & Buybacks

A
Tantalizing
Turnarounds

Terrific Turnaround Profits

Another form of corporate restructuring that can lead to significant investment returns is the successful turnaround. Before clear indications of a turnaround in progress, the company's shares are ignored and even severely depressed as investors respond to continuing bad news. Much earlier, many mutual funds and the vast majority of institutional investors have shed the troubled firm's shares for more promising investment opportunities.

That sets the stage for the individual investor to monitor turnarounds in progress and establish a stake in the distressed security long before Wall Street begins to take notice of the firm's improving operations. For all practical purposes, investing in turnarounds is even more lucrative than investing in IPOs (initial public offerings). You have the same or even greater opportunity to make substantial profits but you don't run the risk of being shut out of investing by heavy demand for the stock as often occurs with IPOs that have drawn considerable public attention. With a turnaround situation, your homework allows you to get in on the ground floor before the institutions begin bidding up the firm's stock market price.

Taking the contrarian approach and ferreting out enticing turnaround investment opportunities can improve your investment returns substantially.

There's another advantage in investing in turnarounds instead of IPOs. Turnaround companies already have an existing line of business that is far easier to evaluate than a new company with a hot idea. Information on the company, key markets, competitors and the industry is readily available while the analysis of IPO company prospects is often based on projections or "guesstimates" which may prove to be wrong to the detriment of the investor.

The focus of the turnaround analysis centers around management and its ability to make the proper decisions to get the company back on track making respectable profits. When clear signs of a successful turnaround in progress reaches Wall Street, investors once again take notice and drive up the company's stock price in anticipation of better days ahead. You could wait until the news hits the financial press and join the herd for the remaining ride or you could do a little bit of upfront investigative work and beat the crowd, earning much greater investment profits.

For example, the naysayers predicted the demise of troubled companies the likes of automotive giant Chrysler Corporation (NYSE: C) in 1980 and copper king Phelps Dodge Corporation (NYSE: PD) in 1984. Patient investors in each of these firms tracked the company and management's progress in turning their firms around and were rewarded with huge investment gains.

Chrysler suffered staggering losses in 1980, sending its stock price below $2 per share (adjusted for stock splits). However, Lee Iacocca redesigned Chrysler's cars and engineered a dramatic recovery in the process. As a result, Chrysler once again became the fast-paced darling of Wall Street. Its stock price soared to $48 per share prior to the October 1987 crash. A $3000 investment for 1000 shares of Chrysler stock would have soared to $106,800 (adjusted for stock splits) for a whopping return 34.6 times the original investment in a period of less than six years.

Chrysler offered turnaround investors another opportunity for substantial gains in the early nineties. After bottoming out near $9 per share in 1991 on a loss of $2.74 per share, Chrysler once again staged a dramatic rebound with steadily improving earnings reaching $10.11 per share in 1994. As a result, investors once again bid up Chrysler's stock price, this time eclipsing its previous high to reach over $63 1/2 per share in early 1994. Declining earnings in 1994 turned investors sour on Chrysler once more, dropping the per share price below $40 per share in early 1995 when Lee Iacocca joined forces with Kirk Kerkorian for a takeover bid for

Chrysler. Interest in Chrysler pushed the stock above $68 per share in May 1996.

Copper producer Phelps Dodge Corporation (NYSE: PD) was fighting for its life in 1984 when copper prices plummeted and combined with high costs to create massive losses and send the company's stock price into a downward spiral bottoming out at less than $6 1/2 per share (adjusted for stock split). After some tough decision making; including moving the firm's headquarters out of New York City to Phoenix, taking on the unions and spending millions of dollars on improved facilities at some plants while shuttering other operations; Phelps Dodge started turning the corner. To be sure, a rebounding economy and rising copper prices also played a major role in the rebirth of the company and its improving fortunes.

By the end of 1986, Phelps Dodge had transformed itself from a high-cost operator into the industry low-cost copper producer. In three years, the firm's stock price had risen more than four-fold to $28 per share (adjusted for stock split) by the October 1987 crash, the year Phelps Dodge earned $2.26 per share.

Of course, the turnaround did not occur in a vacuum. Without an improving copper price environment, Phelps Dodge's rebound would have taken a lot more time and would have been less pronounced. Likewise, the surge in its stock price would not have been as dramatic or as profitable for investors. Therefore, it's critical to keep a pulse on economic activities and forces outside the control of the firm as well as monitoring the company and management's actions.

Like Chrysler, Phelps Dodge enticed turnaround investors a second time. The copper company's stock price declined to around $26 per share (adjusted for stock split) in early 1991 with declining earnings. However, by 1994 management accomplished a near doubling of 1993's $2.66 per share earnings to $5.26 per share and $10.65 per share in 1995. Wall Street responded by bidding up Phelps Dodge's shares to a record high of $70 1/2 per share in mid-1995.

It's obvious that tracking potential turnaround candidates can be significantly rewarding. All of the successful turnaround stories are not relegated to the past. They are part of everyday financial life and going on throughout every year.

"Take a look at the list of top gainers for the previous year. Turnaround companies are consistently among the top performers. In 1995, Applied Magnetics Corporation led the list with a 432% gain, going from under $4 per share to over $18 per share. That was followed by Diana Corporation (+386%) and Continental Airlines (+370%). All of these were turnaround stories. The same holds true for the top performers in 1994 with Rexene Corporation (+313%), Sterling Chemicals, Inc. (+228%) and United Inns, Inc. (+214%)," says Richard L. Evans, a Flossmoor, Illinois independent investment adviser and author of *Finding Winners Among Depressed and Low-Priced Stocks* (International Publishing Corporation).

We will visit some current turnarounds later in this chapter but will first turn to a review of what makes for a successful turnaround and megaprofits for attentive investors.

How to Recognize a Turnaround

Turnaround situations come in many forms. True, the company working itself out of bankruptcy represents an obvious turnaround candidate. However, a firm does not have to be in bankruptcy in order to effect a successful turnaround and deliver substantial investment gains to shareholders and bond holders with the courage to invest when others are fleeing.

As mentioned earlier, the turnaround investor is in a great position to outperform many of Wall Street's institutional money managers. Savvy investors can uncover and track turnarounds in progress and establish their stake before the rest of Wall Street takes notice and jumps on the band wagon, driving up the firm's stock price.

A whole range of circumstances can combine to cause a company's downfall. For example, poor economic conditions can result in a firm's declining revenues and earnings. Firms operating in cyclical industries such as automobile, forest products, mining and steel routinely experience economic contractions which wreak havoc with company operations, profitability and stock prices as clearly illustrated by Chrysler Corporation and Phelps Dodge Corporation. Other outside factors can also negatively impact the firm's ability to compete and result in declining revenues and profits. In the 1980s, the OPEC oil embargo created rapidly rising prices and key raw materials shortages that hurt many companies which could not pass along higher costs to consumers or find substitute materials. New technology and heightened competition in the global market place can also render a firm's product line obsolete or out-of-favor with customers.

Likewise: governmental regulations, as in the case of stricter environmental laws, or the threat of government action such as proposed health care reform can translate to higher costs of conducting business and/or investor concerns over the anticipated negative impact on industry companies, thus driving down stock prices.

California companies are well-familiar with natural disasters such as floods and earthquakes which can temporarily disrupt operations and profits. Shifting consumer preferences from trendy, high-priced goods to value-oriented products or from brand name goods to store brand items can cause customers to flee to other suppliers. On the labor front, George A. Hormel & Company and Deere & Company experience disrupting labor strikes and walkouts almost as a matter of routine.

Ill-planned mergers and failed product introductions can also sabotage company financial results with lost market share and excess costs. Top management can be missing key market opportunities with outdated products and inefficient production facilities while more modern companies reap the benefits. Under-capitalization, excessive debt and poor financial planning and controls come into play with cash flow problems and high cost, non-competitive operations.

However, not all distressed companies represent turnaround situations or the timing may not yet be right for investment. Some firms' operating results and stock prices have been driven down for good reason and without a realistic chance of recovery. On the other hand, companies suffering from a cyclical downturn may still have a way to decline before a turnaround investment is warranted. You need to decipher the cause of the firm's current distressed situation, the prospects of a rebound and the anticipated timing of the turnaround in the company's operating results and subsequent rising stock price.

In its simplest form, a turnaround is a positive change in the fortunes of a company. The firm's improved prospects can derive from a number of internal and external factors. Turnaround candidates provide the chance to earn significant profits from improving developments both within the firm or in its operating or competitive environment. Unlike most other investment situations, the individual investor can learn about potential turnarounds and invest in these special situations before the general investing public and institutions drive up the firms' stock prices.

Since the turnaround occurs over a span of many months to years, you can avoid making rash investment decisions that can devastate your portfolio. Unlike many other investments, with a turnaround you have ample time to perform a thorough analysis prior to committing your money. While declining earnings, poor prospects, negative publicity and uncertainties drive away most investors and force down stock prices you can be working to find the companies with the best chances of recovering over time. The fact that these stocks are avoided by other investors works to your advantage and creates unique opportunities to earn outstanding investment gains.

If many investors had believed that Lee Iacocca would have made Chrysler a winner again, the automobile firm's stock price would never have crashed to less than $3 per share. The uncertainty of the outcome of the turnaround efforts and the looming risk of failure and possible bankruptcy set the stage for enormous gains for those investors willing to investigate and then invest in Chrysler. There are plenty more turnaround situations offering similar lucrative returns.

Contributing to the attraction of turnaround investing, many mutual funds and other institutional investors must refrain from investing in securities which fail to meet their investment guidelines. This places downward pressure on the stock prices of potential turnaround candidates as institutional investors are forced to sell the shares of companies which no longer pay dividends or fail to meet other specific investment criteria. This, in turn, creates significantly undervalued situations for the turnaround investor to capitalize on as the current stock price fails to accurately reflect the firm's underlying value and improving prospects.

Just as institutional selling depresses a company's stock price far below its intrinsic value, as the turnaround company's fortunes improve institutions play a big role in driving the price of the stock upward after it once again passes the investment criteria tests. As operating performance improves, dividends are restored or raised and the financial numbers take on more favorable ratios, attracting portfolio managers desiring to participate in the anticipated rising stock price. This works to the benefit of turnaround investors who established early positions before news of the turnaround in progress became wide spread.

Critical factors make the turnaround a perfect investment vehicle for the individual investor. As illustrated, you can take your time to make a proper analysis of the turnaround prospects. With time on your side, you have access to research material to make a comprehensive, informed decision. In addition, negative publicity has driven down the stock price to new lows, creating undervalued situations and limiting downside risk while you wait for management to mastermind the turnaround or for economic conditions to improve.

Analyzing the Turnaround

Potential turnarounds abound. You can begin your sleuthing for potential investment candidates among the lists of stocks making new lows in financial publications such as *Barron's*, *Investors Business Daily* or the *Wall Street Journal*. Track cyclical companies in industries entering a downturn or approaching the bottom of their current trough. Read business periodicals such as *Business Week*, *Forbes*, *Fortune*, and Standard & Poor's *The Outlook* for listings of companies with low price/earnings ratios or low price/book value compared to their industry or stock market benchmarks.

Since potential turnaround companies typically have suffered earnings declines and/or other financial or operational setbacks, start your search among depressed or cyclical industries in the midst of their economic downturn. Your continual perusal of business and trade publications will alert you to other turnaround prospects.

Recent examples of industries with the potential for rebound include the healthcare, insurance, real estate, technology and utility segments. Likewise, the traditional cyclical industries such as automotive, natural resource companies (building, mining, timber), retailing and steel are ripe ground for the turnaround investor.

Richard Evans pores over the annual "Fortune" ranking of companies that fall in the lower 10% range, especially those stocks which are already trading below $20 per share on the New York Stock Exchange. For example, rebounding companies in 1995 like US Air Group, Inc. (the number one Dow Transportation stock in 1995, up 211%) ranked 393rd, takeover candidate Borden Inc. 394th and Digital Equipment Corporation 386th in the prior year's listing.

"The longer stocks slide the better I like them. They must be on the downtrend at least eighteen months and be off 75% from their highs. You want the stocks to be down long enough so that all the Warren Buffet wannabes have lost patience and sold out," says Evans.

Evans knows what he's talking about. Even Buffet himself abandoned US Air Group at around $6 per share, admitting he had made a mistake.

Actually he made two mistakes, the first one riding it all the way down and then jumping ship near the bottom. One strong sign of support, even with Buffet giving up on US Air, the stock weathered that storm and eventually rose to break through important resistance levels.

"Tracking the support and resistance levels and where people are in the stock is key to successful turnaround investing. Be alert for a change in trend," says Evans.

To accomplish this he monitors trading volumes and stock prices. If a lot of people have purchased US Air Group at $6 per share then it's unlikely that the stock will rise above that level until those people have sold out. Once it pushes through that resistance level then it can move up to the next barrier of shareholders waiting to bail out. However, Evans advises not to be fooled by spike rallies set off by short sellers covering their positions.

Don't forget to keep up with the industry trade publications. Magazines such as *Industry Week, Area Development* and industry specific magazines follow activities of companies on a more timely basis and often in more depth than do the financial journals. You can learn about management changes, plant shutdowns, company spin-offs, new plant construction and other signs of an upcoming turnaround in the trade publications long before they appear in the financial and business press. Searching for turnaround candidates among distressed companies is a bottom-up approach. You can also employ the top-down method of looking at distressed and out-of-favor industries and then zeroing in on specific companies.

Keep track of changes in top management and key operations personnel. Corporate restructuring and major turnarounds frequently begin with a change in executives. Stay alert for announcements of restructurings, sales of divisions or subsidiaries, plant consolidations, mass employee layoffs and large write-offs which provide evidence of management taking drastic action to change the status quo.

A number of factors can trigger a corporate turnaround including the bringing on board of new management talent, research and development creating new technology or a new product introduction, a major new mineral deposit discovery or the signing of contracts for less expensive raw materials, a favorable piece of legislation, global economic expansion, changes in international currency exchange rates and strategic joint ventures or other partnerships.

Target your search on industry giants or small fry with unique market niches. The larger firms can dictate the industry pace and can often create a turnaround by selling off underutilized assets. The smaller firm tends to be more flexible and able to react faster to changing market conditions and opportunities, providing they have access to adequate capital. Middle-size firms, on the other hand, get locked into pricing and policies set by the larger players.

"Give me an average company with excellent management over an excellent company with average management. Management talent will win out over time," says Bradley E. Turner, managing director of Gradison-McDonald Asset Management in Cincinnati, Ohio.

New or expanded management ranks send the signal that the company's board of directors is serious about making changes to improve the company's operating and financial results and, as a result, the firm's stock price. It's not a no-holds buy alert but it is a strong indication that you should begin tracking the success or failure of management's actions.

The financial press and trade magazines keep good tabs on shakeups in management or the addition of new management talent. Follow this action closely. When companies bring new executives on board, check into their credentials and experience with reviving a distressed company. Estimate whether or not their industry and/or financial experience is up to the job at hand. Iacocca had a reputation of no-nonsense management and demanding the best results from those around him. If anyone could prevent Chrysler from driving over the precipice and maneuver the automotive company back on track, Iacocca was the one. His selection was a major signal to investors that a Chrysler turnaround moved from a very remote possibility to one with a serious, however slim, chance of succeeding.

Don't give up on a company if management does not change or get an influx of new talent. Often, the dire circumstances of the company is enough for management to admit past mistakes and set down the road of taking corrective action to turn their firms into more prosperous operations. Many top executives own substantial blocks of shares and have options to acquire more stock. Obviously, they are not happy about the company's depressed stock price either and will make every effort to correct the situation. When you get right down to it, they also have their jobs on the line. That should provide plenty of inspiration to strive hard for improved results.

In addition to taking a good hard look at management, it's important to assess the financial strength of the company. Does it possess the financial resources and banking relationships to continue in business? Are cash flow, working capital and bank lines of credit sufficient to keep the doors open while management takes corrective action? The company's bankers, creditors and bond holders play a pivotal role in the ultimate success or failure of the turnaround. Determine if they are willing to work with the company or are taking an adversarial position. There's no sense spending valuable analysis time if the firm's financial viability is in serious question.

Once the management team and company finances have passed the smell test, it's time to determine the probability that company earnings can make a successful rebound. This involves analyzing reasons for the firm's misfortunes. Is an economic contraction, industry cycle or a product life cycle at the root of the problem and how will anticipated changes in those scenarios impact the company and its ability to bounce back? Don't lose sight of the fact that some distressed companies will fail or never return to former heights.

This part of the analysis takes a look at what new management strategies are in the works and their likelihood of success. Determine if new acquisitions appear well planned or represent a shotgun approach to new market realities. Ask what new and innovative marketing avenues management is attempting to regain market share. Look at the changes to determine whether or not the actions taken are designed to create a new vibrant company or are merely cosmetic stopgap measures to buy time.

Evaluate each of the company's crucial operations from manufacturing to marketing and from finances to research and development to get an understanding for how well the company is handling problem areas. Equally important, get a feel for how external factors such as a prolonged economic slowdown can impact the firm's operational and financial standing. After all, no matter how efficient a company becomes, if the economic environment forecasts a continued dropping off of sales, the company will be unable to stage a robust recovery. Remember, no company can "save itself into prosperity."

Keep a pulse on the competitive and regulatory environments as well. For example, jurisdictional bodies in the United States could take an even harder stance on gaming operations. Instead of just failing to approve new gaming facilities, as has happened in some states, they could institute new and higher tax measures on gaming companies. Even more severe, politicians and jurisdictions could react to growing public pressure against gaming and greatly restrict new gaming facilities or even rescind existing gaming licenses.

Acquiring the Analysis Tools

Now it's time for you to take action and obtain the analysis tools to help you make the right investment decision. Call the shareholders services or investors relations department and request copies of recent quarterly company financial reports and press releases. Also ask for copies of the last three years annual reports and 10Ks to get a pattern of how things have progressed over time.

These will let you know management's assessment of the situation, what actions have been taken to date and what troublesome operational and financial areas to be aware of in your analysis. Another required SEC report, the 8K details information on specific occurrences such as the acquisition or disposition of assets, changes in the certifying accounting firm, director resignations and other materially important items.

The financial reports often carry management's analysis and interpretation of industry trends and overall economic scenarios. Read the general business and financial publications and trade magazines to form your own independent opinions and to guard against management's blue-sky approach in the face of impending disaster. Remember, often it's the same management team who steered the company into its current mess. For a broader picture of the industry and competitive situation obtain copies of competitors' reports and perform the same analysis. Compare operating and financial ratios for industry companies of similar sizes. *The RMA Annual Statement Studies* published by Robert Morris Associates in Philadelphia, Pennsylvania is a handy tool for accomplishing this valuable comparison. The RMA publication lists key ratios by industry and size firm. The ratios include:

— Cost of sales
— Coverage-dividend
— Coverage–interest
— Expense to sales
— Leverage
— Liquidity
— Operating

The RMA Annual Statement Studies provides industry trend data for a 5-year period and a directory of other sources of composite financial data for more than 225 industry classifications. A ratio by itself does not give a lot of information. For maximum utility, it must be compared to other company or industry ratios and tracked over time to determine trends and changes in direction. When analyzing the company's financials for clues to the turnaround, ferret out the real reasons for and the consequences of write-offs. In many cases, they represent non-cash charges and don't negatively, and often positively, impact corporate cash flow and future earnings potential. Restructuring charges signal that management recognizes problem areas and is taking action to correct the situation. Likewise, while nobody likes to see people laid off, employee terminations or middle management buyouts help trim company fat and make the company more efficient as long as the cutbacks are properly reviewed and don't hurt ongoing operations.

There's plenty of readily accessible independent and objective information on companies you want to analyze for investment consideration. Start with your public or university library for copies of the *Value Line Investment Survey* and Standard & Poor's *The Outlook* for relatively current information. In addition, there are plenty of subscriber investment newsletters that specialize in turnaround and special situations. *The Turnaround Letter* is published monthly by New Generation Research, Inc. The subscription rate is $195 per year. For information write to 225 Friend Street, Suite 801, Boston, Massachusetts 02114 or call 617-573-9550. *Charles M. LaLoggia's Special Situation Report and Stock Market Forecast* can be obtained for an annual subscription rate of $230 or a 3-month trial offer of $79. This newsletter covers a number of special situation topics included in this book including stock buybacks, undervalued stocks, possible takeover candidates, spin-off companies and insider trading. It is published every 3 weeks by CML Market Letter. You can contact the newsletter at P.O. 167, Rochester, New York 14601 or call 800-836-4330.

The ball is in your court. Do your homework and earn the substantial investment gains that turnaround situations deliver year after year. Analyze all of the elements that could impact the corporate turnaround and then make an informed decision to buy or not. To aid in your decision making process the following case studies illustrate the traits of successful and unsuccessful turnaround candidates.

Putnam's Pick

"Investing in turnarounds is attractive for several reasons. First of all, it's a fairly inefficient market niche that most institutions stay away from because they have been burnt on the way down as the company's fundamentals fell apart. Second, most traditional investment analysis tools that institutions use such as book value, earnings per share and price/earnings ratios are not useful since they are negative in many turnarund cases. Third, there is substantial upside investment gain potential," says George Putnam III, editor of *The Turnaround Letter*.

At the present time Putnam likes the prospects of some of the airline companies as turnaround prospects, particularly Trans World Airlines, Inc. (AMEX: TWA).

TRANS WORLD AIRLINES, INC.

One City Center
515 N. Sixth Street
St. Louis, MO 63101
314-589-3000
AMEX: TWA
S & P Rating: NR

Company Profile. Trans World Airlines, Inc. once ranked as the world's premier transatlantic air passenger carrier. The industry deregulation of the 1980s and fierce competition took its toll on TWA. A debt-laden takeover by Carl Icahn in 1985 compounded the airline's problems and in 1992 TWA filed for Chapter 11 bankruptcy from which it emerged in November 1993. However, operating results once again were insufficient to carry the heavy debt load and TWA plunged into bankruptcy for a second time in June 1995. This time the company emerged out of Chapter 11 in August 1995.

Financial Statistics.
($ millions except per share and ratio data)

	1993*	1994	1995**
Working Capital	N/A	(1279)	(111)
Revenues	N/A	3408	3316
Net income (loss)	N/A	(436)	(227)
Long-term debt	N/A	340	1023
Per share data	1993	1994	1995
Earnings (loss)/share	N/A	(22.54)	N/A
Dividends/share	—	—	—
Stock price range/share	1993	1994	1995
High	6 7/8	5 1/2	14 5/8
Low	4 1/8	1/2	4

* Company reorganized late 1993
** Includes eight months results of predecessor company and reorganization costs.

Company Strengths. According to Putnam, TWA has dramatically cut its expenses, transforming itself from one of the highest cost airlines to one of the lowest. TWA has also focused its operations around two efficient and competitive hub systems in St. Louis and JFK Airport in New York City. This time it appears that TWA has pared down its debt load to manageable levels. Employees take a strong interest in the airline's prosperity with 30 percent ownership of the outstanding shares and representation on the Board of Directors. The company has brought together an industry experienced executive team under the leadership of Chief Executive Officer Jeffrey Erickson.

Investment Analysis. Airline industry conditions continue to improve with strong travel demand working to reduce disruptive cutthroat competition. Another plus, reduced foreign subsidies level the playing field.

"We feel TWA has got it right this time around. There's still significant risk that a downturn in the industry could severely hurt TWA but the appreciation potential definitely outweighs the risks at this time. TWA's improved prospects have not gone unnoticed; Fidelity announced that it had acquired 7 percent of the stock in early 1996.

Turnarounds in the Making

EnviroSource Inc.

P.O. Box 10309
5 High Ridge Park
Stamford, CT 06904-2309
203-322-8333
NASDAQ: ENSO
S & P Rating: C

Company Profile. EnviroSource Inc. is a leading, long-term supplier to industrial customers of specialized services principally involving the recycling, handling, stabilization or landfilling of environmentally sensitive wastes or byproducts. A restructuring of operations in 1993 and an infusion of capital through recapitalization is beginning to pay dividends.

Financial Statistics.
($ millions except per share and ratio data)

	1993	1994	1995
Working Capital	(17)	(8)	(34)
Revenues	271	260	265
Net income (loss)	(46)	11	10
Long-term debt	236	260	275
Per share data	1993	1994	1995
Earnings (loss)/share	(1.44)	.26	.20
Dividends/share	—	—	—
Selected ratios	1993	1994	1995
Debt ratio	.87	.87	.87

Stock price range/share	1993	1994	1995
High	5 1/8	4 1/2	4 3/4
Low	2 1/2	2 3/4	2 1/2

Company Strengths. A more focused EnviroSource has turned in a profit for two years in a row after disposing of unprofitable operations in 1993. Likewise, the 1993 recapitalization used stock and bond sale proceeds to retire higher cost debt and improve financial and operating flexibility.

Investment Assessment. High operating rates at many of EnviroSource's customers mean increased demand for its services. A cost reduction program is also adding to bottom line results. While the still high debt level remains a concern, the improved operating performance and future prospects make EnviroSource a tantalizing turnaround candidate. At one time the company's stock traded as high as $16 1/2 per share but only commands around $4 per share currently. Assuming a year of earnings improvement in 1996, EnviroSource's stock price could break through the $4 3/4 per share resistance level and deliver substantial investment gains.

LAIDLAW INC.

3221 N. Service Road
Burlington, Ontario, Canada L7R 3Y8
905-336-1800
NYSE: LDWB
S & P Rating: B+

Company Profile. Laidlaw Inc. is a North American leader serving government, industry and individuals with transportation and environmental management services. Earnings peaked in 1990 at $1.10 per share and tapered off to 34 cents per share by the end of fiscal 1993 (non-recurring charges resulted in an overall loss of $1.05 per share in fiscal 1993). Disposal of its European operations, increased emphasis on the high-growth healthcare transportation business and three major acquisitions in 1995 appear to have put Laidlaw back on track to higher profits.

108

Financial Statistics.
($ millions except per share and ratio data)

| | Fiscal Years Ended August 31 | | |
	1993	1994	1995
Working Capital	246	221	167
Revenues	1993	2128	2517
Net income (loss)	122	91	133
Long-term debt	1377	1403	1669
Per share data	1993	1994	1995
Earnings (loss)/share	.34	.37	.48
Dividends/share	.12	.12	.12
Selected ratios	1993	1994	1995
Percent earned net worth	7.9	6.8	7.8
Percent net margin	6.1	5.1	5.3
Stock price range/share	1993	1994	1995
High	9 1/2	8 1/2	10 1/4
Low	5 3/8	5 1/2	7 5/8

Company Strengths. Laidlaw's aggressive acquisition program has improved its market posture in both hazardous waste (with the purchase of Union Pacific's hazardous disposal business) and transportation (with the acquisition of Mayflower, the U.S.'s second largest bus operator). Laidlaw leads the North American industry in hazardous waste management and school bus transportion and ranks third in solid waste management. The diversification move into health care transportation rounds out the company's transportation services.

Investment Assessment. Laidlaw Inc. is on track to post a better than 20 percent earnings increase for fiscal 1996 and beyond. At $10 per share the stock is trading at less than half of its 1991 high of $20 1/4 per share. Considering that Laidlaw is making twice the earnings achieved in 1991 the stock is a good long-term holding for capital gains as the turnaround continues.

SANIFILL, INC.

2777 Allen Parkway
Suite 700
Houston, TX 77019
713-942-6200
NYSE: FIL
S & P Rating: B

Company Profile. Unlike Laidlaw Inc., Sanifill specializes in non-hazardous waste collection and disposal operations. It owns and operates disposal and treatment facilities in more than 20 states. Originally started in 1990 as a disposal only company, the firm moved into the collection end of the business in 1992 and this operation now generates approximately 25 percent of annual revenues. The strategic move also turned around earnings which had declined more than 25 percent in 1992.

Financial Statistics.
($ millions except per share and ratio data)

	1993	1994	1995
Working Capital	—	1	—
Revenues	121	173	257
Net income (loss)	12	19	58
Long-term debt	144	188	270
Per share data	1993	1994	1995
Earnings (loss)/share	.83	1.12	1.40
Dividends/share	—	—	—
Selected ratios	1993	1994	1995
Percent earned net worth	8.6	10.5	9.0
Percent net margin	10.3	10.9	12.1
Stock price range/share	1993	1994	1995
High	22 1/8	25 5/8	34 1/8
Low	13 1/4	20 1/8	22 3/8

Company Strengths. Sanifill is on the upswing again with a redirection of its operations more toward waste collection activities. Likewise, a number of acquisitions are expanding waste collection operations as well as landfill, transfer sites and materials recovery facilities.

Investment Assessment. Earnings are on a strong rebound from their low in 1992 and hit a record high of $1.40 per share in 1995, a 25 percent boost from the previous year. With another 20 percent rise in earnings projected, 1996 looks to be another banner year. The stock price has been hitting new highs as investors gain increased confidence in Sanifill's ability to keep the turnaround in tact.

SENSORMATIC ELECTRONICS CORPORATION

500 N.W. 12th Avenue
Deerfield Beach, FL 33442-1795
305-420-2000
NYSE: SRM
S & P Rating: B+

Company Profile. Sensormatic Electronics Corporation manufactures and services electronic surveillance systems and individual article theft control devices and systems. The company represents an angel fallen from favor. The once darling of Wall Street ran into a buzzsaw of accounting problems, restated earnings, lower earnings per share and resulting lack of investor confidence.

Financial Statistics.
($ millions except per share and ratio data)

	1993	1994	1995
Working Capital	176	140	127
Revenues	487	656	889
Net income (loss)	54	72	70
Long-term debt	265	151	144

Per share data	1993	1994	1995
Earnings (loss)/share	.97	1.16	1.02
Dividends/share	.20	.22	.22
Selected ratios	1993	1994	1995
Percent earned net worth	11.0	9.9	7.3
Percent net margin	11.1	11.0	7.8
Stock price range/share	1993	1994	1995
High	35	39 1/4	38 1/4
Low	20	26	16 1/4

Company Strengths. Sensormatic Electronics operates in a fast growing market sector as corporations tighten security and retail operations seek innovative ways to reduce theft of their goods. In the wake of the accounting and other problems the company moved fast to bring in R. Vanourek as its new president. Vanourek has a reputation for turning companies around and installing tight financial and operating controls. He has already trimmed the company's work force by 7 percent in efforts to get costs under control.

Investment Assessment. Management is making the right moves to get Sensormatic turned around but it may take awhile to regain investor confidence after a dramatic restatement of earnings and stock price drop from a high of $38 1/4 per share in 1995 to $13 5/8 per share. The stock has partially rebounded to the $19 per share level. Of course there's plenty of work to be done before Sensormatic regains its former position. The uncertainty over whether or not Vanourek and his team can pull off the turnaround makes for potentially significant investment gains. Sensormatic is surely a company to keep your eyes on in the weeks and months ahead as the restructuring continues.

SMITH INTERNATIONAL, INC.

16740 Hardy Street
Houston, TX 77032
713-443-3370
NYSE: SII
S & P Rating: B-

Company Profile. Smith International, Inc. is a leading supplier of products and services to the global oil and gas drilling, production and mining industries. Major business segments include drill bits, fluids and remedial drilling services and down-hole tools.

Financial Statistics.
($ millions except per share and ratio data)

	1993	*1994*	*1995*
Working Capital	182	257	300
Revenues	221	654	875
Net income (loss)	68	36	46
Long-term debt	46	115	117
Per share data	1993*	1994	1995
Earnings (loss)/share	1.79	.92	1.16
Dividends/share	—	—	—
Selected ratios	1993	1994	1995
Percent earned net worth	7.4	14.2	15.2
Percent net margin	7.2	5.5	5.2
Stock price range/share	1993	1994	1995
High	11 1/2	17 5/8	23 7/8
Low	7 7/8	8 3/8	11

* Includes nonrecurring charges and gains

Company Strengths. Smith International, Inc.'s turnaround is more dramatic than it appears on the surface because the $1.79 per share earned in

113

1993 includes a one-time gain of $73.6 million or $1.95 per share from the sale of its discontinued Directional Drilling business partially offset by charges of $19.9 million or 53 cents per share for a litigation settlement and $1.3 million or 3 cents per share for accounting changes. After a decade low level of drilling activity industry experts anticipate a rise in the demand for drilling services as large international oil companies seek to replenish their dwindling reserves as world wide energy use increases. Smith International is in a prime position to benefit from such a scenario.

Investment Assessment. Look for better bottom line results as drilling activity boosts revenues and Smith International's improving margin enhances earnings per share comparisons. Rising earnings gave the stock the strength needed to push through the $23 per share resistance level on an upward surge to $30 per share.

STRUCTURAL DYNAMICS RESEARCH CORPORATION

2000 Eastman Drive
Milford, OH 45150-2789
513-576-2400
NASDAQ: SDRC
S & P Rating: C

Company Profile. Structural Dynamics Research Corporation, like Sensormatic, was a high-flying company shot down by improper accounting practices, subsequent restatement of earnings and class action lawsuits. The company is a leading international supplier of mechanical design automation software, engineering services and product data management software. The company's stock price hit a high of $30 per share in 1992 before troubles sent the stock on a downward spiral below $4 per share in late 1994.

114

Financial Statistics.
($ millions except per share or ratio data)

	1993	1994	1995
Working Capital	27	28	36
Revenues	148	168	204
Net income (loss)	(12)	(13)	(8)
Long-term debt	—	10	8
Per share data	1993	1994	1995
Earnings (loss)/share	(.39)	(.45)	(.28)
Dividends/share	—	—	—
Selected ratios	1993	1994	1995
Percent earned net worth	—	—	—
Percent net margin	—	—	—
Stock price range/share	1993	1994	1995
High	21 5/8	17 1/8	30 1/2
Low	9 5/8	3 5/8	5 1/8

Company Strengths. During the fourth quarter of 1995, Structural Dynamics took a nonoperating charge of $22.6 million, settling securities class-action lawsuits. This clears the way for Structural Dynamics to refocus all of its efforts on the business of running the company. On an equally positive note, the company enjoys excellent business relationships with major clients such as Ford Motor Company which recently signed a five-year $200 million technology agreement with Structural Dynamics.

Investment Assessment. The troubles are in the past and the recent $30 million acquisition of CAMAX Manufacturing Technologies adds additional depth to Structural Dynamics' capabilities and technology. Its stock price has rebounded strongly to $28 7/8 per share. In early February 1996 Morgan Stanley upgraded its coverage of Structural Dynamics. A return to profitability in 1996 will complete the turnaround cycle and should bring even higher stock prices.

TransTexas Gas Corporation

1300 East North Belt
Suite 310
Houston, TX 77032
713-987-8600
NASDAQ: TTXG
S & P Rating: NR

Company Profile. TransTexas Gas Corporation is one of Texas' largest independent natural gas producers and marketers. The company went public in March 1994 with an initial public offering priced at $14 per share. TransTexas carries on an active drilling program in South Texas and other areas.

Financial Statistics.
($ millions except per share and ratio data)

	Fiscal Years Ended July 31*		
	1993	*1994*	*1995*
Working Capital	(57)	(9)	107
Revenues	326	336	313
Net income (loss)	94	24	(69)
Long-term debt	83	500	800
Per share data	1993	1994	1995
Earnings (loss)/share	.75	.33	(.93)
Dividends/share	—	—	—
Selected data	1993	1994	1995
Proved reserves (Bcfe)	707	729	1141
Average finding cost ($Mcfe)	1.01	1.12	.46
Stock price range/share	1993	1994	1995
High	—	14 1/8	21
Low	—	10	9 3/8

* In 1996, TransTexas changed its fiscal year end to January 31.

Company Strengths. TransTexas Gas Corpration has extensive industry experience having drilled more than 1,400 wells, with a completion rate exceeding 80 percent, since 1973. Discoveries of two new natural gas fields near Laredo boosted company reserves by 56% in fiscal 1995 to more than 1.1 trillion cubic feet. Lower finding costs have improved Trans Texas's position as a low cost operator. The company has instituted gas commodity hedges designed to mitigate gas price risk. Approximately 56 percent of fiscal 1996 production is hedged. Disposal of noncore assets will bring in needed operating cash. Despite a 29 percent decline in natural gas prices, Trans Texas was able to stem its cash flow decline to only 5.5 percent. The fiscal 1995 repurchase of its $500 million 10 1/2% notes and issuance of $800 million of 11 1/2% notes extends the maturities and provides the company with the funds to develop new discoveries.

Investment Assessment. As with any turnaround situation, TransTexas has its share of risks. Continued lower gas prices will hamper revenues and earnings and maintaining adequate cash flow will be critical to the company's success. On the positive side, TransTexas possesses substantial reserves and property with the potential to substantially increase revenues, cash flow and earnings as natural gas prices recover. There are two ways to play TransTexas. The common stock trades around $10 per share, less than one half of its 1995 high of $21 per share. As the earnings picture begins to improve, the stock should trend higher. For those desiring income you might consider the 11 1/2% Senior Notes of 2002 with a first call date of June 15, 2000 at 105.75.

Assessing Your Own Turnarounds

There are a few caveats to consider before investing in your own turnaround candidates. First and foremost, make sure you do your upfront homework and investigate before you invest. Study the past three years' annual reports to see where the problem areas are and what management is doing to correct the situation. Review the economic condition of the industry and its prospects over the next few years as the turnaround unfolds. Likewise, analysis the competitive situation. Can the company realistically regain market share from bigger, stronger industry competitors?

Once your analysis is done and you feel comfortable that the company is poised for recovery it's time to take a position. There are a number of ways to accomplish this and it depends on your own investing style and risk parameters. For most investors purchasing the common stock gets the most bang for your buck. However, more conservative and income oriented investors may opt for debt obligations of the company. Check to see if the company has any outstanding convertible or preferred securities that can deliver current income and allow you to participate in the outside potential of the underlying common stock. You may even earn a windfall if the convertible or preferred issues are cumulative and the company has stopped paying dividends on them. When conditions improve, the cumulative dividends in arrears will have to be paid to those shareholders before any dividend on the common stock can be reinstated or initiated.

The ball's in your court. Search out turnaround candidates in cyclical or distressed industries, stock market sectors currently out-of-favor with the investing public and companies which are rebounding from past mistakes or outside events which have negatively impacted their operating and financial results and stock prices.

You, too, can earn substantial investment profits by uncovering these turnaround treasures, performing your analysis and assuming a measured degree of risk. Happy hunting.

B

Successful
Spin-Offs

Cashing in on Corporate Castoffs

Savvy investors have been making megabucks investing in companies that many other investors shun. Along with the record breaking pace of mergers and acquisitions as discussed in Part 1, companies have been spinning off divisions, subsidiaries and other operations at a breakneck pace. In 1993 alone, $26 billion in spin-off activity took place, up from $4.25 billion in 1992. There have been more than 200 new spun-off companies hitting the street and attracting investors since 1992. According to Securities Data Company of Newark, New Jersey a record 81 spin-offs took place in 1995, up substantially from 48 in 1994.

While companies have been engaging in spin-off activity for decades, there is a dramatic change in the reasons underlying the strategy. In the past; many spin-offs were regarded as, and were in fact, "dogs" which management wanted to shed in order to improve corporate operating results, earnings and the company's stock price. Therefore most investors were attracted to the more focused corporate parent while the spin-off generated little if any investor attention.

Spin-off activity stretches across the broad spectrum of industries. Likewise, it encompasses the spin-off of a wide variety of operations from small divisions to major subsidiaries. It can also take the form of a major company splitting itself into two or more parts as evidenced by the breakup of AT&T with over $80 billion in annual revenues into three new companies: AT&T Communications, Global Informations Systems and Lucent Technologies. The goal is for all three businesses to perform more efficiently and profitably as separate entities than they did as a single unit. In addition, the breakup will remove AT&T from competition with a number of its major customers. It's a case where the parts should be worth a lot more than the whole.

Illustrating the wide variety of spin-offs from which to chose, other recently completed or announced spin-offs include Baxter International Inc.'s decision to dispose of its hospital-supply business, Dun & Bradstreet Corporation's move to split itself into three separate publicly traded companies, Host Marriott Corporation spinning off its concessions business and Roadway Services Inc. action to spin off of its largest subsidiary, Roadway Express, Inc. The spin-off investment prospects are virtually endless. The largest announced spin-off in 1995, based on disclosed dollar value, was General Motors Corporation's decision to spin off its Electronic Data Systems unit to shareholders. The Electronic Data Systems deal is worth $21 billion. The largest completed 1995 spin-off was the $9.3 billion transaction involving U.S. West Inc. spinning off US West Media Group to shareholders.

Spin-Off Research

Independent research by professors in the early 1990s at the Graduate School of Business at University of Texas in Austin and the Smeal College of Business Administration at the Pennsylvania State University at University Park, Pennsylvania documented that spin-offs represent excellent opportunities to make higher-than-normal investment returns. To be sure, not every spin-off company will go on its own to perform well and achieve higher revenues and earnings. However, investors willing to spend a little investigative time to separate the promising spin-offs from the "dogs" stand to profit handsomely for their efforts. The evidence also points out that investing in the restructured parent companies can also payoff with superior investment returns.

The comprehensive research indicates that spin-offs significantly outperform the market during the first three years their shares are traded. The University of Texas study conducted by associate professor of finance Keith

C. Brown and Van Harlow, a vice president with Fidelity Management Trust Company in Boston, reviewed a sample of 74 spin-off events covering a 10-year span beginning in January 1980. The Brown and Harlow research evaluated the impact of institutional investors shedding their shares in spun-off companies in order to rebalance their portfolios and stay within their specific investment guidelines. The new shares may not meet the investment policy of institutional investors in terms of credit constraints, industry exposure or liquidity and force the investment manager to shed the stock.

Often, the forced liquidations generate substantial, but temporary, downside pressure in the stock prices of the spin-off companies. Earlier research by Seifert and Rubin (1989) concluded that newly created spin-off shares experienced abnormal losses by as much as 10 percent in the first several months after their initial trading. The downward price pressure initiated by institutional selling due to investment policy considerations took place without regard to the spin-off companies' future prospects.

Brown and Harlow's data confirmed that there is a tendency for institutional investors to substantially reduce their spin-off holdings after a corporate restructuring. For a sizable number of spin-off firms, this reduction leads to a significant, seller-induced stock price drop. The key for spin-off investors is that this downward price pressure is temporary. On top of that, the scope of the initial price decline and subsequent stock price rebound were both significantly linked to the extent to which institutional investors liquidated their spin-off positions. In other words, the greater the pressure of institutional sales on spin-off shares, the steeper the initial price decline and the more dramatic the price rebound. This pattern presents unique investment opportunities for alert investors to earn substantial profits from taking stakes in promising spin-off companies.

Brown and Harlow uncovered some telltale signs that the tendency for institutions to sell their spin-off shares could be explained to some extent by investment constraints that could be observed in advance, the most notable being the presence of the parent firm in the Standard & Poor's 500 index.

Research performed by Patrick J. Cusatis of Lehman Brothers in New York City and James A. Miles and J. Randall Woolridge of the Smeal College of Business Administration at Pennsylvania State University found new evidence that spin-offs create value. The study evaluated 161 tax-free spin-offs covering 27 industries over the 1965-1990 time frame.

As reported in the Summer 1994 issue of the Journal of Applied Corporate Finance (Volume 7, Number 2), Cusatis, Miles and Woolridge calculated growth rates for a number of key variables such as net sales, operating income before depreciation, capital expenditures and total assets to determine the effects of the spin-offs on operating performance. The study showed that prior to the spin-off the parent companies exhibited substandard operating performance. However, after the spin-off, consolidated results exhibited improved results for the parent company and greatly improved performance for the spun-off subsidiaries. In fact, the spin-off companies experienced very rapid growth in all of the key accounting variables studied.

Turning to stock market performance, the study found that despite poor operating performance during the years prior to a spin-off, the stock market performance of the parent companies during the two years leading up to the spin-offs was quite good. For the 24 months prior to the spin-off ex-date, the parent companies' stock earned an average return of about 31 percent in excess of the market over the same time period. The major proposed reason for this seeming anomaly is that the spin-off is part of a larger ongoing restructuring program designed to improve the parent company's overall operating performance. In effect, the stock market has already factored in the anticipated favorable outcome of the company's restructuring activities. After the spin-off the parent companies exhibited excess returns for the one-year, two-year and three-year periods of 12.5 percent, 25.7 percent and 18.1 percent, respectively.

Likewise, market returns for the spun-off companies were analyzed and compared with market returns over various time frames. During the first six months spin-off company returns trailed by 1 percent. By the end of one year the situation reversed and spin-off companies earned an excess of 4.5 percent. The stock market discrepancy increased as spin-off companies went on to earn excess returns of 25.0 percent after two years and 33.6 percent after three years.

A number of reasons are presented to account for the improved performance of spin-off companies including greater decision making authority, management performance incentives and less bureaucratic layers hampering operations. Stock market performance is also enhanced by a significant number of takeovers of both spin-offs and the parent companies. At least two-thirds of the spin-off companies were operating in businesses unrelated to their parents' main lines and were acquired by firms in businesses related to their own. Cusatis, Miles and Woolridge concluded that both the parent companies and their spin-offs were five times more likely to be taken over than other companies.

In comparison to IPOs, which investors over-enthusiastically bid up in price and routinely earn negative abnormal returns for up to the three-year period following the initial public offering, spin-offs offer above average returns over the three year period as the downside pressure of institutional selling tapers off and the firm's underlying favorable prospects come to light. As discussed, much of the negative stock market price pressure has little to do with the intrinsic value and potential of the spin-off firm and mainly results from institutional investment policies.

Cusatis, Miles and Woodridge list a number of reasons for spin-offs outperforming their IPO counterparts. First of all, the initial IPO stock price surge tends to adjust downward as reality sets in. Next, spin-off company organizational changes start to deliver improved operating performance. Third, investors anticipate or recognize the superior operating and generate additional demand for the company's stock, boosting per share prices. Finally, as indicated earlier, a number of spin-offs become takeover targets of other industry firms.

Searching Out Attractive Spin-Off Candidates

Astute investors tracking spin-off activity can earn significant investment profits by purchasing the shares of well-positioned parent companies and their spin-off orphans. Without a doubt, not all spin-off investments turn out to be success stories but the research shows that the odds are in your favor to earn substantial above average gains by paying attention to the world of corporate spin-offs and investigating enticing parent and spin-off companies before their stock prices run up.

Spin-off investing represents one of those market niches where the individual investor can outperform Wall Street with a little bit of investigative legwork and analysis time. Take the contrarian view and purchase good value spin-off candidates while they are still out of favor with the big institutional money. Then rake in the investment profits after the investment managers wake up to the spin-offs' true potential and bid up their stock prices.

"It's hard for big diversified companies to get sponsorship by Wall Street due to the variety of businesses and industries they operate in. Dramatically different growth rates of their operations make them hard to analyze. Therefore, there's a lack of adequate analyst coverage for the parent company and the spin-off companies are often under-followed at first," says Bradley E. Turner, managing director of Gradison-McDonald Asset Management in Cincinnati, Ohio.

For the most part, spin-off companies have a hard time getting their story told. Typically, they are dumped on the market with a scarcity of information and little if any following. Unlike their IPO counterparts, there are no high pressure underwriters touting their strengths and beating the bushes for investors. In addition, information on the spin-off company's prior operating history as part of the parent company and even its main lines of business remain buried in the parent's consolidated financial statements. Documents relating to the soon to be independent company are often only available upon request.

While the lack of information and understanding of the firm's business cause the spin-off company to be ignored by most research analysts and major market players, that's exactly the reason individual investors can take advantage of the undervalued spin-off special situation. It creates a unique opportunity for those investors willing to do some investigative and analysis work on their own.

As the majority of companies get over-analyzed by a number of analysts and investors, the spin-offs and their parents often get ignored. It only makes sense that you won't be able to ferret out superior investment opportunities on companies being covered by a dozen or more research analysts. New companies, such as spin-offs, remain under followed and represent real opportunities for uncovering hidden value and earning significant portfolio profits.

"The spin-off can create a way for the parent company to refocus on its strengths and high growth businesses while the spin-off company can become more entrepreneurial and profitable. Investors can decide which piece, the parent or the spin-off, best fits their investment goals and risk parameters," says Turner. Spin-offs and their parent companies get undervalued for several reasons. As indicated above, they may be ignored by investment analysts. The spin-off company may be avoided because it's believed that the parent company is getting rid of a poor performing operation with poor future prospects. Likewise, the industry sector in which the spin-off company operates may be faced with slow growth or be out-of-favor with Wall Street.

In reality, there's a host of other, valid reasons firms spin-off a division or subsidiary to company shareholders. A takeover threat, the need to raise capital, and tax considerations may come to play a role in management's decision making process. Diversified companies often fail to achieve their true valuation by the market and use the spin-off as a way to unlock the hidden value and enhance shareholder return. Justifications for other spin-offs include cutting loose operations either too small or not closely aligned with the parent's major lines of business.

Even if the spin-off is cut loose due to its slow growth or money losing operations that doesn't mean you should ignore it. In this case, you view it as a turnaound situation with the prospect of delivering substantial investment gains. Removal of restrictive headquarters rules and an infusion of new capital, equipment and human resources can be the impetus for the company to turn the corner. A spin-off managerial team can create an entrepreneurial spirit that works wonders for the bottom line.

One only needs to look at Freeport-McMoRan Inc. (NYSE: FTX) to find a classic undervalued situation uncovered by the spin-off process. As part of its restructuring; Freeport-McRoRan separated its two principal businesses, agricultural minerals and copper/gold operations, into two independent entities. Freeport-McMoRan owns over 50% of Freeport-McMoRan Resource Partners, L.P. (NYSE: FRP), the world's largest phosphate producer. The restructuring included the spin-off of its interest in Freeport-McMoRan Copper& Gold Inc. (NYSE:FCX) on a tax-free basis on July 17, 1995.

The move made both companies' operations more focused and was designed to provide better access to credit markets and reduced financing costs. Another part of the restructuring included the sale of 21.5 million shares of FCX Class A common stock to RTZ Corporation for $450 million. The proceeds were used to pay down Freeport-McMorRan outstanding debt. The restructuring process was announced by management over a year earlier, giving investors plenty of time to investigate and evaluate which company or companies to invest in.

One way I participated in the restructuring of Freeport-McMo-Ran Inc. was to purchase the 6.55% convertible subordinated bonds. Trading around

$910 per $1,000 bond as recently as December 1994, the convertible bonds delivered an attractive yield in excess of 7 percent while I waited for the market reaction to management's restructuring moves. Prior to the spin-off of its mineral unit, Freeport-McMoRan called in the bonds. I opted for converting to the common shares and rode the stock price up for a capital gain. After the July 1995 spin-off, Freeport-McMoRan's stock price rose from a low of $24 per share to a 52-week high of $44 1/2 per share (taking into account a reverse six-for-one split). Likewise; the shares of spin-off Freeport-McMoRan Copper & Gold, Inc. performed well, rising from $20 per share in mid-1995 to hit a high of $34 7/8 per share in early 1996. The market also found favor with Freeport-McMoRan's primary holding of Freeport-McMoRan Resource Partners, L.P., boosting its stock price from $16 per share in mid-1995 to a 52-week high of $22 3/4 per share in early 1996.

As illustrated, the spin-off announcement provides plenty of time to perform your analysis and take a position to earn significant investment gains. Freeport-McMoRan's restructuring efforts began years earlier even before the spin-off of the minerals operation was announced. In fact, the company had already spun-off its oil and gas exploration operations in mid-1994, setting the stage for a major corporate restructuring. Savvy and patient investors earned a decent yield while waiting for the restructuring to unfold and then large capital gains on the stock price rises in shares of the Freeport-McMoRan companies.

"Search out companies that are unconglomerating and unbuckling themselves. Companies with a variety of unrelated businesses suffer in the market which tends to reward pure plays. That's one reason the uncovering of hidden values as companies spin-off operations generates positive market reactions," says Charles M. LaLoggia, publisher of *LaLoggia's Special Situation Report and Stock Market Forecast* in Rochester, New York.

LaLoggia suggests tracking companies in the Diversified Companies section of *The Value Line Investment Survey* for potential spin-off candidates. The same holds true for diversified industry classifications in the chemical, insurance, metals & mining (such as Freeport-McMoRan) and natural gas segments. Taking a global approach, the Value Line Diversified European section bears some consideration.

A quick perusal of Value Line's Diversified Companies section brings to light a number of names recently making headline news. For example, Figgie International, Inc. (NASDAQ: FIGIA) is investigating various alternatives to sell or split up the conglomerate which produces products ranging from air purifiers to life support systems to military electronics. Within the past year, Teledyne, Inc. (NYSE: TDY) has been an active acquirer and the subject of an unwanted takeover bid by WMX Technologies, Inc. (NYSE: WMX) as a result of its over-funded pension plan. In early April 1996, Teledyne agreed to a $3.2 billion merger with Allegheny Ludlum Corporation (NYSE: ALS).

LaLoggia finds WMS Industries (NYSE: WMS) intriguing as a potential spin-off situation with the shedding of its hotel properties in Puerto Rico. Recent operating and earnings per share performance has been dampened by poor performance at the hotel operations. WMS Industries' earnings declined to 80 cents per share in fiscal 1995 ended June 30, 1995 from $1.19 per share in fiscal 1994.

According to LaLoggia, WMS has approximately 80 percent of the market share for arcade, pinball and video games and is moving into the casino arena. For the first half of fiscal 1996, earnings have rebounded to 38 cents per share versus 21 cents per share for the first six months of fiscal 1995. With the gaming industry out-of-favor, better earnings comparisons and a potential successful spin-off of its hotel segment in the works, WMS industries could represent an attractive portfolio holding as well as a lucrative takeover target that could deliver substantial investment gains. It is important to note that Sumner M. Redstone, Chairman of Viacom, Inc. (AMEX: VIA) owns approximately 25 percent of WMS Industries' outstanding shares. WMS Industries' stock rebounded in May 1996 from the low end of its 52-week price range of $24 per share to $16 per share to reach $20 1/8 per share.

Analyzing the Orphans

More than a year can pass from the time the parent company announces a proposed spin-off until the shares of the spin-off company are distributed. Few analysts and institutional research companies are willing to spend time and money analyzing a potential spin-off which may not materialize and for which they may be little, if any, institutional interest. Therefore, many spin-offs come to market with relatively little analysis information or analysis. This lack of information, coupled with the negative price pressure as institutions dump their undesired spin-off shares, creates a unique investment opportunity for the individual investor.

To get started in spin-off investments keep abreast of upcoming spin-offs. *Barron's*, *Investor's Business Daily* and *The Wall Street Journal* regularly cover spin-off announcements. In addition, business magazines such as *Business Week*, *Forbes* and *Fortune* periodically provide more in-depth coverage of spin-off companies and their parents. Read the industry trade magazines such as *Industry Week* and industry specific journals to get a feel for which firms are expanding, contracting or restructuring their operations. The trade publications typically cover restructuring stores in advance of the general business and financial press. Studying the trades will give you a jump on other investors.

Once you are hot on the trail of potential spin-offs, contact the parent company for details on the proposed spin-off. The firm's corporate or public relations department will send you a copy of the SEC required Information Statement, SEC Form 10 which includes a five-year history of the newly created company. Request to be placed on the press release list to keep informed on how the spin-off is progressing.

Reviewing this material will give you a wealth of information for your spin-off analysis. The SEC Form 10 includes data on the spin-off company's main lines of business, business history, business properties, affiliated companies, competition, depth of management experience, amount of director and executive participation in company ownership, financial and debt structure, liquidity and capital resources. Analyzing these factors can give you a good picture of the company's potential prospects and future operating results.

Look for competitive advantages that can give the spin-off company an edge over industry competitors. Is the company a low-cost industry producer or control important raw materials sources? Does it possess innovative patents or trademarks? Does its market niche permit it to charge and receive premium pricing for its products or services? Investigate how its margins and other key ratios compare with industry standards. Are they improving or declining? Do high entry costs prevent additional competition from entering the industry picture in the future? Does it have the financial resources to capitalize on the industry's consolidation either through strategic acquisitions and/or aggressive marketing actions to garner additional market share?

Determine whether capital expenditures are keeping the company's plant and equipment and production processes efficient. Have the research and development efforts paid off with successful new product development?

Does the firm's future depend on a few major customers or government contracts susceptible to the budget cutting process? How does management view the competitive market situation? Are current work backlogs rising or declining? Does the firm have alternative raw material sources to alleviate production interruptions or escalating raw material prices? How will cyclical economic forces impact future operations and profitability?

How has the company dealt with labor? Is the company unionized and what is the history of labor strife disrupting operations? Will the company be able to implement cost cutting strategies without incurring extended and costly work interruptions?

Make a thorough review of the financial statements. Are cash reserves and cash flow adequate to fund needed capital expenditures, research and development and market expansion? Are costs holding steady or rising? Is the company debt-heavy with debt servicing expenses that hurt cash flow and earnings potential? How secure are the company's lines of credit and banking relationships? Does the company depend on high-cost financing or are the interest rates it pays comparable to industry averages? Analyze extraordinary charges or credits to determine whether or not they are truly one-time events or can come back to hurt future earnings potential. Has the company successfully assimilated past acquisitions and made penetrations into new markets? Look for write-offs associated with ill-planned and executed acquisitions, new product introductions and other failed attempts to gain market share.

Evaluate how external forces can impact the spin-off company's operations. Will the firm take on significant legal liabilities as the result of the spin-off? How can environmental issues and government regulations impact the firm's cost structure or ability to remain a competitive force in the industry?

Analyzing competitor and industry trends helps you gain insight into how the spin-off company fits into the picture. Request copies of competitor annual reports and Form 10Ks. Compare their financial performance in terms of revenues, costs of goods sold, administrative and selling overhead, margins and net income with that of the spin-off firm. Look for differences in capital structure and debt load and how that impacts the spin-off company's competitive position.

Pay close attention to Management's Discussions of Operating Results to get a fix on each company's perspective of major industry trends and the major issues facing the industry. Are they similar or on opposite ends of the spectrum from the views of other industry leaders? Investigate reasons for the differences. Evaluate which firm's strategies appear most reasonable in light of industry trends and therefore most likely to succeed over the long-term. Your trade magazine reading will put you in position to make a good analysis.

By keeping well-informed on factors that can affect your spin-off company and its chances of success you enhance your odds of choosing the right investment candidates to earn superior returns. Remember, investigate before you invest. Finding the answers to the above questions will help you ferret out top investment performers in both spin-offs and their parent companies.

Super Spin-Offs

The following announced and completed spin-off situations provide a good starting point for beginning your own analysis in order to enjoy significant investment gains. In addition, a list of other spin-offs recently in the news will give you a host of other leads. The rest is up to you.

DUN & BRADSTREET CORPORATION

187 Danbury Road
Wilton, CT 06897
203-834-4200
NYSE: DNB
S & P Rating: A

Company Profile. Dun & Bradstreet is a premier information services company functioning in several business segments. Its Moody's Investors Service publishes financial information and issues bond ratings. The A.C. Nielsen subsidiary performs market research and measures television audiences. Reuben H. Donnelley ranks as the largest publisher of "Yellow Pages" telephone directories. Dun and Bradstreet Information Services markets a number of innovative information systems such as portfolio analysis software. The company maintains an increasing global presence with over 40 percent of annual revenues deriving from outside of the United States.

Financial Statistics
($ millions except per share and ratio data)

	1993	1994	1995
Working capital	78	(206)	196
Revenues	4710	4896	5415
Net income (loss)	595	630	321
Long-term debt	—	—	—
Per share data	1993	1994	1995
Earnings (loss)/share	.23	3.70	1.89
Dividends/share	2.40	2.56	2.63
Selected ratios*	1993	1994	1995
Percent earned net worth	61.7	47.7	56.0
Net Profit margin	14.5	12.9	11.9
Stock price range/share	1993	1994	1995
High	68 1/2	64	65 1/2
Low	55 3/4	51 7/8	48 1/2

*Based on earnings before extraordinary charges

Company Strengths. Revenue is growing at double digits rates. Dun & Bradstreet is a leading company in each market it serves. The late 1996 split of the company into three parts aims at unlocking franchise strengths and maximizing shareholder value. Currently, the company pays a dividend yielding better than 4 percent. While this may be slightly reduced as a result of the spin-offs, it should be attractive in relation to other stocks.

Investment Assessment. The company's 1995 results include charges of $1.91 per share related to the breakup of the company into three pieces. The company will spin-off its A.C. Nielsen market research unit and the newly created Cognizant Corporation, which will provide marketing information to the pharmaceutical and healthcare industries as well as audience measurement services and advisory services.

"Dun & Bradstreet is a conglomeration of different businesses not fully valued in the market. The three pieces should command $10 to $15 more per share after the breakup. The company is one of a handful with more than 40 years of back-to-back dividend increases," says Bill Staton, Chairman of The Staton Institute for America's Finest Investors in Charlotte, North Carolina. The stock trades in the mid-range of its 52-week price range of $69 per share to $50 1/2 per share.

EASTMAN CHEMICAL COMPANY

100 North Eastman Road
P.O. Box 511
Kingsport, TN 37662
423-229-2000
NYSE: EMN
S & P Rating: NR

Company Profile. An early 1994 spin-off from Eastman Kodak Company, Eastman Chemical is a leading international producer of chemicals, fibers and plastics. Its products are used in a wide variety of applications including adhesives and coatings, inks, nutrition and formulation products, resins, soft drink containers and other packaging such as shrink packaging.

Financial Statistics
($ millions except per share and ratio data)

	1993	1994	1995
Working capital	634	473	559
Revenues	3903	4329	5040
Net Income (loss)	(209)	336	559
Long-term debt	1801	1195	1217
Per share data	1993	1994	1995
Earnings (loss)/share	N/A	4.05	6.89
Dividends/share	N/A	1.20	1.62

Selected ratios*	1993	1994	1995
Percent earned net worth	19.2	25.9	32.5
Net profit margin	5.2	7.8	11.1

Stock price range/share	1993	1994	1995
High	48 1/8	56	69 1/2
Low	42 7/8	39 1/2	48 1/2

*1992 ratios based on proforma information after spin-off from Eastman Kodak Company

Company Strengths. Eastman Chemical management has turned the spin-off company around, boosting revenues substantially and reporting record earnings for 1995. There's more in store for the years ahead, especially if the economy heats up. The firm is gearing up for that possibility by expanding its worldwide production capacity between 5 and 10 percent in 1996. Strong cash flow will provide the capital for additional expansions and market penetration.

Investment Assessment. Projected earnings for 1996 and 1997 are $7.20 per share and $7.70 per share, respectively. An announced $400 million stock buyback program will further enhance earnings per share comparisons. This is on the heels of the completion of a $200 million share repurchase program in 1995. See the discussion of the impact of stock buybacks later in Part 2.

The stock hit a high of $76 per share in 1996 before retracing below $70 per share in April 1996. This may be a reaction to the problems confronting the tobacco industry, which uses Eastman Chemical's filter tow products in the manufacture of cigarettes, or it may be in reaction to brief takeover rumors in early 1996.

The stock offers a double play based on projected higher earnings in the years ahead and as a potential takeover target. Purchase for the long-term for superior capital gains possibilities.

THE GEON COMPANY

6100 Oak Tree Boulevard
Cleveland, OH 44131
216-930-1000
NYSE: GON
S & P Rating: NR

Company Profile. The Geon Company ranks as one of North America's largest manufacturers of PVC resin for use in construction and automotive products. It carries on global operations from 13 manufacturing plants in the United States, Canada and Australia. Geon came to market as a $1.2 billion spin-off from B.F. Goodrich in April 1993.

Financial Statistics
($ millions except per share and ratio data)

	1993	1994	1995
Working capital	25	48	64
Revenues	973	1209	1268
Net income (loss)	1	57	32
Long-term debt	88	93	93
Per share data	1993	1994	1995
Earnings (loss)/share	.04	2.01	1.24
Dividends/share	.375	.50	.50
Selected ratios	1993	1994	1995
Revenue growth	8.7	24.2	5.0
Stock price range/share	1993	1994	1995
High	24 3/8	31 5/8	31 3/8
Low	17 3/4	23 1/4	23 3/8

Company Strengths. Despite lower earnings in 1995, as the result of lower spreads between resin prices and raw materials and substantially reduced fourth quarter shipments, Geon has achieved a dramatic turnaround from its pre-spin-

134

off days of 1991 when the company lost $135 million on $1.2 billion in revenues. Looking ahead; long-term debt refinancing, consolidating operations and a streamlined product line bode well for reductions in costs over the long-term.

Investment Assessment. The 1995 results don't look as bad as they first appear. The numbers include nonrecurring charges of $39.1 million or $1.51 per share. An improved cost structure and increased VCM manufacturing production capacity coming on line in 1996 will bolster earnings in 1996 and beyond. With Geon's stock trading under $28 per share, near the middle of its 52-week price range of $31 3/8 per share to $23 3/8 per share, there's room for a rebound on higher earnings performance in the months ahead.

THERMO INSTRUMENT SYSTEMS INC.

81 Wyman Street
P.O. Box 9046
Waltham, MA 02254
617-622-1111
AMEX: THI
S & P Rating: NR

Company Profile. Thermo Instrument is taking the lead of its parent Thermo Electron Corporation (NYSE: TMO) and creating its own flurry of spin-off companies. The 1986 spin-off produces analytical instruments used to measure and detect air pollution, radioactivity and toxic substances. An active and successful acquirer, Thermo Instruments is now in the spin-off mode with sales of minority interests in ThermoSpectra in 1994, Thermo BioAnalysis and ThermoQuest in 1995 and the November 1995 announcement to spin-off Thermo Optek.

Financial Statistics
($ millions except per share and ratio data)

	1993	1994	1995
Working capital	238	230	400
Revenue	584	662	765
Net income (loss)	45	60	77
Long-term debt	286	264	340

Per share data	1993	1994	1995
Earnings (loss)/share	.50	.63	.88
Dividends/share	—	—	—
Selected ratios	1993	1994	1995
Percent earned net worth	12.5	13.7	14.5
Net profit margin	7.7	9.1	10.1
Stock price range/share	1993	1994	1995
High	18 5/8	18 1/2	27 1/8
Low	12 1/4	14 1/2	15 7/8

Company Strengths. Thermo Instrument continues to benefit from its previous spin-offs due to majority interests in them. The company continues to make earnings per share gains around 20 percent. Improving cash flow will keep new products in the pipeline and Thermo Instrument on the acquisition trail. Management has proven itself adept at improving the operations of acquired companies and penetrating new markets. Recent acquisitions make Thermo Instrument the world's top analytical instrument manufacturer as well as the leading producer of environmental instruments.

Investment Assessment. Thermo Electron still holds 83 percent of Thermo Instruments' outstanding shares so a relatively small increase in demand can translate into large stock price rises. Projections for 1996 push earnings past the $1.00 per share level.

The company has been a solid market performer. Its stock has skyrocketed from under $2 per share in 1986 to a high of $38 3/8 per share in May 1996 (adjusted for stock splits). See discussion of stock splits later in Part 2. Thermo Instrument is a solid long-term pick for above average returns. Don't overlook its parent or spin-off companies as prospective investments for capital gains.

BONUS SPIN-OFF CANDIDATES

Company	Exchange/Symbol	Comment
Albemarle Corp.	NYSE: ALB	Specialty chemical manufacturer spin-off from Ethyl Corporation, improving earnings picture
AT&T Corp.	NYSE: T	Breakup into three parts to unleash creativity and eliminate business conflicts
Baxter Inter.	NYSE: BAX	Uncoupling of former merger viewed favorably, higher earnings in store
Dial Corp.	NYSE: DL	Another conglomerate unbundling, rebound in earnings will help stock price
H & R Block	NYSE: HRB	The one to watch here is spin-off CompuServe
Lexmark Intl.	NYSE: LXK	1991 IBM LBO came to market in 1995, produces laser and inkjet printers, excellent growth potential
Melville Corp.	NYSE: MES	Separate retail units promise to perform better than the whole, CVS will be holding company's earnings engine
Minnesota Mng	NYSE: MMM	More focused 3M to deliver higher earnings

Premark Intl.	NYSE: PMI	A 1986 spin-off from Dart & Kraft, Premark intends to spin-off high growth Tupperware, track both
Sprint Corp.	NYSE: FON	Spin-off of 360 Communications will be second largest domestic cellular pure play
Transport Holdings	NASDAQ: TLIC	Travelers spin-off targets niche insurance market and key acquisitions

Not All Spin-Offs are Made in Heaven

George Putnam warns that while the research shows that spin-offs usually increase shareholder value this is not always the case. He points to INTERCO Inc.'s (NYSE: ISS) spin-off of its Converse and Florsheim footwear businesses as a prime example. Before the November 1994 spin-off INTERCO's stock closed at $14 per share. Earnings declined substantially in 1995 and the stock dropped to $5 1/2 per share before rebounding a bit. Likewise, Converse Inc. (NYSE: CVE) lost money in 1995 and its stock plummeted to a low of $3 1/2 per share from a 1994 high of $12 5/8 per share. Don't just rush out to purchase spin-off companies without doing your investigative work. One poor investment can wipe out months of hard earned gains.

Not all proposed spin-offs come to market. Anheuser-Busch Companies came to the realization that it could not effectively compete in the snack business against the Pepsi's of the world. Anheuser originally tried to sell its Eagle Snacks Inc. unit but finally opted to shutter the business and sell its plants to rival Frito-Lay Inc. and incur a $206 million write-off. In addition, Anheuser spun off its Campbell Taggart Inc. bakery operation in early 1996 to shareholders under the new name, Earthgrains Company (NYSE: EGR). With two years of operating losses and tough industry competition, the bakery spin-off does not appear too appealing. However, a more focused Anheuser-Busch could turnaround operations and return revenues and earnings to former growth rates.

Specialized Spin-Off Information Sources

The Spin-off Report is an independent research publication that issues in-depth research reports, valuations and investment recommendations on individual subsidiaries about to be divested as new publicly traded companies. *The Spin-off Calendar* provides continuous coverage of all newly announced spin-offs and spin-offs in progress. Both are published by Hunstrete Corporation, 55 Liberty Street, 9th Floor, New York, New York 10005 ,212-233-0410. The subscription rate is $10,000 annually and includes both reports and consultation. The reports are also available through The Bear Stearns Companies Inc.

Rothchild Inc. in New York City publishes *The Spin-off Monitor*. The investment research report is available at a subscription rate of $12,000 or $20,000 in trading commissions. Rothchild Inc. can be contacted at 1251 Avenue of the Americas, New York, New York 10020 or call 212-403-3500.

Barbara Goodstein, a senior vice president at Rothchild, conducted a study of 60 tax-free spin-offs between 1991 and 1994. She found that the spin-off shares appreciated 28.2%, vs. 16.5% for NASDAQ stocks and 10.3% for the Standard & Poor's 500-stock index.

C
Stock
Splits

The Stock Split Scenario

Normally, stock splits abound in bull markets as the result of surging stock market prices. According to the *New York Stock Exchange Fact Book*, 1983 marked the watermark year with a record 300 stock splits taking place on the New York Stock Exchange. Other high years in recent history include 272 stock splits in 1986 and 244 in 1987. Ironically, the current bull market saw stock splits drop from 181 in 1993 to 131 in 1994 before rebounding in 1995 as the stock market broke new ground and surged ahead to penetrate the 5000 level for the first time in history during November 1995 (See Chart 2-1).

Several theories abound for the reduced level of stock splits in the midst of the greatest bull market ever. One proposition is that stock splits tend to lag the increase in share prices due to the time required by companies to split their shares. If so, the rapid rise in stock prices during 1995 could be followed by a boost in the number of stock splits in 1996 and beyond.

Second, the heavy pace of mergers and acquisitions as well as companies spinning off operations or breaking themselves into several pieces with lower stock prices could also be a damper on the number of stock splits taking place. In fact, you could consider corporate spin-offs as the ultimate stock split. Finally, some boards of directors are avoiding stock splits to keep down the number of shareholders and thus reduce administrative costs associated with shareholder services.

New York Stock Dividends and Splits, 1985-1994

Year	Less than 25%	25% to 49%	50% to 99%	2-for-1 to 2 1/2-for 1	3-for-1 to 3 1/2-for 1	4-for-1	Over 4-for-1	Total
1994	15	6	35	62	10	1	2	131
1993	21	18	52	87	3	0	0	181
1992	18	9	55	87	10	2	1	182
1991	18	8	33	46	1	0	1	107
1990	25	7	19	49	2	0	3	105
1989	28	9	34	66	2	2	1	142
1988	34	11	29	25	4	1	0	104
1987	36	18	59	118	10	1	2	244
1986	43	22	78	118	9	1	1	272
1985	40	17	43	60	6	0	0	166

Chart 2-1. (Source: *New York Stock Exchange Fact Book* 1994. Used with permission of the New York Stock Exchange, Inc.)

Stock Split Basics

Just what is the initial impact of a stock split? Think of it this way. On the surface, a stock split does not change your financial stake in the company. Your ownership percentage of outstanding company shares remains the same after the split as it did before the stock split took place, only now each share is worth less. Economically, you are not any better off now then you were before, you just have more pieces of paper representing the same ownership.

Consider the following analogy. If I give you two $10 dollar bills in exchange for your $20 dollar bill, your cash value remains the same at $20 even though you have doubled the pieces of paper representing your $20 in value. A two-for-1 stock split works the same way. There is no increase in value resulting from the stock split transaction itself.

To illustrate further, assume the following data for ABC Inc.:

Outstanding Common Stock	1,000,000 shares
Par Value Per Share	$1
Market Price Per Share	$40
Dividend Payout Ratio	25%
Net Income	$5 million

From this data, we can calculate a number of key pieces of financial information. First of all, earnings per share work out to $5 per share ($5 million/1 million shares). Next, cash dividends total $1.25 million ($5 million x .25) or $1.25 per share ($1.25 million/1 million shares).

If you were fortunate to own 1,000 common stock shares of ABC Inc., the market value of your investment would total $40,000 (1,000 x $40 per share). Your ownership percentage of the company would be 1/10th of 1 percent (1,000/1,000,000).

ABC's board of directors votes to declare a 2-for-1 stock split. In other words, every shareholder would receive two shares of ABC common stock for each share of company stock they own on the date of record. When the stock split takes place a doubling of outstanding shares occurs and each outstanding share after the split now has a market value or split-adjusted price of $20 versus the pre-split price of $40 per share value.

The financial impact of the ABC Inc. 2-for-1 stock split is illustrated below:

ABC Inc.

Outstanding Common Stock	2,000,000 shares
Par Value Per Share	$.50
Market Price Per Share	$20
Dividend Payout Ratio	25%
Net Income	$5 million

Earnings after the stock split comes in at $2.50 per share ($5 million/2 million shares) since there are twice as many outstanding shares. Dividends still total $1.25 million but the per share rate also drops in half to the $.625 per share level.

Your portfolio now owns 2,000 shares of ABC Inc. common stock worth $40,000 (2,000 x $20 per share), the same market value as prior to the stock split. Likewise, your ownership percentage of the firm remains at 1/ 10th of 1 percent (2,000/2,000,000). Your 2,000 shares still deliver the same amount in cash dividends as before with $1,250 ($.625 x 2000).

As you can see, the above financial evidence illustrates that the stock split transaction results in neither a gain or a loss. Your stake in the company is exactly equal to that as before the split. Given that the above is true, then why do stock splits attract so much investor attention? The answer to that lies in market research involving stock splits and market reactions to splits. The research uncovers some interesting theories on the impacts of stock splits on investor sentiment and stock prices.

Stock Split Realities & Theories

While the stock split itself may not deliver any financial gain to the shareholder, accompanying events do create situations which create additional value that can translate into significant investment gains. First of all, as stock prices rise to lofty levels they tend to get beyond the purchase range of many individual investors. A stock split is designed to reduce the company's stock price and once again place it within a reasonable price range. This action can create additional demand for the company's stock and demand drives stock prices.

Individual investors may be more willing to purchase 400 shares of a $40 stock for an investment of $16,000 versus buying only 200 shares of the same company at an $80 stock market price. Not only can you purchase more shares but the commission charges get spread over more shares, permitting you to recoup investment expenses faster and enhance your investment return.

New York Stock Exchange statistics also seem to support the theory that individual investors prefer to acquire stocks in reasonable price ranges. Despite a prolonged bull market in the eighties and early nineties, the average share price tended to adjust itself downward after price runups.

"Most individual investors are hesitant to make initial stock purchases or add to existing positions once a stock sells above the $75 per share range. Individuals like to purchase round lots. It's no accident that the average price for shares listed on the New York Stock Exchange tends to hover around the $35-to-$40 per share range," says Robert Stovall, president of Stovall/Twenty-First Advisers Inc. and an adjunct professor of finance at New York University's Stern Graduate School of Business.

Management also likes stock splits since the increase in the number of shares after a stock split broadens the company's shareholder base, making the firm less susceptible to price swings caused by traders and institutional investors. A broad shareholder base can also be a deterrent to unwanted takeover bids. Stock splits are popular with growth companies which desire to conserve capital for use in expanding the business instead of paying out cash dividends. The assumption is that cash used to fund operations, research and development and strategic acquisitions will enhance shareholder value more than cash dividends.

Many consumer oriented and service companies use stock splits to increase their shareholder base as a means to boost revenues. New shareholders represent an untapped market for the company's products and services.

"Often the stock split is accompanied by a boost in the cash dividend, raising the yield the shareholder receives on his or her holdings. This creates extra value and helps raise the stock price after a stock split," says Bradley E. Turner, managing director of Gradison-Asset Management in Cincinnati, Ohio.

The stock split is also a signal of good news. After all, the stock split would not have occurred in the first place if the company's stock price had not risen dramatically based on good earnings performance or at least the prospects of better times ahead. The approval of a stock split also represents a vote of confidence by the board of directors that management can keep its record of improving operating and financial results on track. The anticipation of increased earnings and dividends can add a lot of fuel to the company's stock price.

There's also a direct correlation between the number of shareholders and the number of analysts that follow a stock. The better the coverage by Wall Street analysts, the more incentive for dealers to make a market in the stock. This translates to increased liquidity, smaller price spreads and higher demand...all positives for the stock price.

The Empirical Evidence

A number of research studies evaluating the impact of stock splits on stock prices have been conducted. According to a New York Stock Exchange study, stocks which have split appreciate 2 1/2 times faster than stocks which have not split, for up to seven years after the split.

Early stock split research performed by Fama, Fisher, Jensen and Roll (FFJR) and reported in *International Economics Review* in February 1969; found that the New York Stock Exchange stocks studied during the period from 1927-1959 exhibited sharp price increases prior to a split. The FFJR study concluded that investors purchasing stocks after their splits would earn normal returns. Later, Reilly and Drzycimski confirmed that investors earned higher than normal returns up to three trading weeks before the announcement date but no abnormal returns after that date.

More recent studies paint a very different picture. Grinblatt, Masulis and Titman research in 1984 concluded that stock prices, on average, react positively to stock split announcements (and dividend announcements) that are not contaminated by other simultaneous announcements such as earnings releases and merger information. Research by Ohlson and Penman indicated a 30 percent increase in the return standard deviations after the ex-split date which were not temporary.

As reported in the July 1989 issue of *The Accounting Review*, Paul Asquith and Krishna of the Harvard Business School and Paul Healy of the Massachusetts Institute of Technology's Sloan School of Management concluded that significant corporate earnings increases exist in the four years prior to the stock split announcement. These earnings increases appear to be permanent since the earnings changes after the stock split announcement are either insignificant or positive for up to five years. Pre-split earnings increases stem from both industry and company-specific factors.

Firms that announce stock splits tend to be in industries which perform well, but outperform their industry counterparts in the year prior to the split date. The stock price reaction to stock split announcements is related to the firm's earnings increases in the two years prior to the splits, consistent with the belief that split announcements lead to an upward revision in investors' probability assessments that pre-split earnings increases are permanent rather than temporary.

David Ikenberry (Rice University's Jesse H. Jones Graduate School of Administration), Graeme Rankine (American Graduate School of International Management) and Earl K. Stice (Hong Kong University of Science and Technology) released a stock split study in January 1996 which evaluated 1,275 two-for-one stock split declarations between 1975 and 1990. IRS concluded that splits are motivated by both the company's desire to maintain a stock price trading range and based on favorable expectations regarding future performance. As a result, stock split announcements are indirectly informative to investors.

IRS also determined that the market on average underreacted to stock split announcements. Although the mean announcement return came in at 3.38 percent, the initial reaction is biased downward. The stocks of split firms experience an additional permanent excess gain of 7.94 percent in the first year after the declaration and after three years the compounded excess performance increases to 12.14 percent. Comparisons were made with companies of similar size and book-to-market ratios.

Firms splitting to relatively low post-split prices or firms with poor pre-split performance exhibit weak post-split performance. Obviously, the stock split cannot hide poor underlying fundamentals.

Moving from the academic arena to real world investing, in 1995 Ford Investor Services, Inc. in San Diego, California evaluated the truth or fallacy of a number of popular stock split investment rules. Using 20 years of stock split history in the Ford Data Base, researchers calculated returns for the month, quarter, six months and one-year periods following the stock split. The stock split adages tested included the following:

Sell...reverse splits do not entice institutional investors
Sell...only if greater than 3-for-2 because it is too dilutive
Buy....lower prices attract more buyers
Sell...additional shares create distribution

The results are tabulated in Chart 2-2.

147

Relative Performance 12/74 to 12/94 (%)

| Event | Time Period Following Stock Split | | | |
	Month	Quarter	6 Months	Year
Reverse Split	-1.44	-3.31	-2.79	-6.98
No Split	-0.02	-0.03	-0.04	-0.04
Stock Dividend	2.18	1.01	0.86	1.20
Three-for-two	1.83	3.33	4.37	4.39
Two-for-one	2.05	3.53	5.21	5.45
Three-for-one	1.63	1.27	0.06	0.32

Chart 2-2. (Source: Used with permission of Ford Investor Services, Inc.)

Some of the rules appear to be borne out by the evidence. For example, the 43 reverse splits in the Ford Data Base under performed the universe across all time frames. The research also pointed out that splits up to and including two-for-one outperformed the universe in all time frames. Three-for-two and two-for-one splits showed the best relative performance from six-months to one-year from the splits. Above two-for-one splits seemed to limit the performance to the month and quarter of the splits.

Looking at specific numbers, after a year two-for-one splits outperformed the universe by 5.45 percent while three-for-two splits delivered an above average return of 4.39 percent. The three-for-one split starts out with a return advantage of 1.63 percent which nearly disappears by the end of six months. The reverse split starts out with a negative performance of 1.44 percent after one month and goes down hill from there, ending up with a negative performance of 6.98 percent after twelve months.

Ecogen Inc. (NASDAQ: EECN), a developer of biological pesticides, learned the reverse split rule the hard way. Its late January 1996 announcement of a one-for-five reverse split, which would reduce the company's outstanding shares from over 34 million to approximately 7 million, was greeted by the market with a 15 percent stock price drop to $6 5/8 per share in heavy trading. By early April, Ecogen's stock lost another 24 percent to $5 per share.

Of course, there are exceptions to every rule. Freeport-McMoRan Inc., which we discussed earlier in Part 2, executed a six-for-one reverse split after spinning off its metals operation and the stock performed nicely.

148

For the individual investor, the major point of all of the above is that boards of directors vote stock splits because they believe in the continuation of the company's operating results and improving earnings and dividends. It's your job to determine when this optimism is warranted. Stock splits provide testimony to a company's track record of successfully delivering revenue and earnings gains plus enhanced shareholder investment returns via rising dividends and higher stock prices. The stock split investor must be able to discern which managements can lead their companies to even higher operating results while taking into account economic, industry and competitor information. Use the stock split as a warning to be alert for more earnings gains and higher stock prices in the months and years ahead. But investigate before you invest.

Tracking stock split companies after the announcement is one way to capitalize on the opportunity for higher than normal investment returns. Obviously, if you can ferret out upcoming stock split candidates and invest in them before the announcement date, you gain an additional edge and put yourself into position to earn more impressive returns, assuming you pick the right candidates.

Where to Find Attractive Stock Split Candidates

In this regard, you can research companies that have a record of successful operations and a past history of stock splits and accompanying cash dividend increases. Remember, if you're investing in the company for the long-term, make sure it has strong enough fundamentals to keep the revenue, earnings and dividend growth on track after the split.

"The Dow 30 is a good place to start. It is loaded with a number of companies trading above $80 per share. Already in 1996, AT&T has announced its decision to split itself into three companies and Coca-Cola has voted a two-for-one stock split," says Robert Stovall.

Stovall also suggests looking at industries which have performed well in the recent bull market. For example, the pharmaceutical industry sports Merck, Pfizer and Warner-Lambert with prices ranging from $60 to over $100 per share.

Stovall's column in *Financial World* routinely discusses stock splits each Spring and includes a list of companies possibly on the verge of splitting. Among companies mentioned in his May 20, 1996 column were American International Group which split later in 1995 and which we analyzed in Part 1. Other companies on Stovall's 1995 list include Emerson Electric and Unilever NV both of which we covered in the merger section of this book.

Where else do you look for promising stock split companies? Obviously, companies with a history of splitting their stocks are good prospects. Seek out firms whose boards of directors have split their shares several times in the past. They already possess experience initiating and completing stock splits and are aware of the benefits to their stock performance.

The *New York Stock Exchange Fact Book* provides a listing of all Big Board companies with stock splits during the prior year. It is a good starting point for searching out companies with a track record of stock splits. The *New York Stock Exchange Fact Book* can be obtained by sending $10 to The New York Stock Exchange, Inc., Eleven Wall Street, New York, New York 10005.

In the same vein, *The Value Line Investment Survey*, Standard and Poor's tear sheets and *Standard & Poor's Dividend Record* are excellent places to initiate your investigation. All are found in most community and university libraries. Standard & Poor's *The Outlook* also reports on stock splits and the prospects of potential stock split candidates. A subscription to *The Outlook* runs $298 per year. Standard & Poor's can be contacted at 25 Broadway, New York, New York 10004 or telephone 212-208-8000. The *Value Line Investment Survey* costs $570 per year but Value Line Publishing, Inc. routinely offers a $55 trial subscription. Value line Publishing, Inc. is located at P. O. Box 3988, New York, New York 10008-3988 or call 800-833-0046 for subscription information. Look for other special offers in the financial press such as *Barron's, Investors' Business Daily* and *The Wall Street Journal*.

Additional handy resources include *Moody's Handbook of Common Stocks, Moody's Handbook of Nasdaq Stocks, Hoover's Handbook of American Business*, the *American Stock Exchange Fact Book* and the *Nasdaq Fact Book & Company Directory*, the last three published by The Reference Press, Inc. Moody's Investors Service can be reached at 99 Church Street, New York, New York 10007 or call 800-342-5647. The Reference Press, Inc. can be contacted at 6448 Highway 290 E, Suite E-104, Austin,

Texas 78723 or call 800-486-8666. Much of the above material can also be accessed via computer databases. Inquire about details with the appropriate publisher.

The *United & Babson Investment Report* published by Babson-United Investment Advisors, Inc. periodically offers a bonus report on stock split candidates for new subscribers. The Fall 1995 special research report included the stocks in Chart 2-3 which United & Babson considered favored for new buying. The *United & Babson Investment Report* offers a special subscription rate of $149 for six months ($268 annually) which includes several bonus research reports on various topics such as "Growth Stocks to Buy Now," "U.S. Companies with a Global Reach" or "Buy-Hold-Sell on 85 Utility Stocks." For information write to *United & Babson Investment Report*, Babson-United Building, 101 Prescott Street, Wellesley Hills, Massachusetts 02181 or call 617-235-0900.

Eight Promising Stock Split Candidates

Company	Est. 1995	Earnings Per Share 1994	52-Week Price Range	Recent Price	P/E Ratio	Div.	% Yield
Avon Prod.	$4.10	$3.75	75-54	72	18	$2.20	3.1
Chubb Corp.	6.90	5.50	97-69	94	14	1.96	2.1
Emerson El.	4.60	4.05	75-58	70	15	1.96	2.8
Fd. Nt. Mtg.	8.55	7.77	108-68	107	13	2.72	2.5
Ga.-Pac.	12.00	3.28	96-66	86	7	2.00	2.3
LG&E Ener.	2.95	2.90*	41-36	40	14	2.22	5.6
Norfolk So.	5.45	4.90	77-59	73	13	2.08	2.8
Roy. Dutch	8.40	6.76	128-105	125	15	4.63	3.7

Notes: P/E ratios calculated based on recent price divided by estimated 1995 earnings. Emerson Electric year September of following calendar year and per share 1994 is estimated amount. * From continuing operations. Chart 2-3 (Source: used with permission of Babson-United Investment Advisors, Inc.)

Emerson Electric and Georgia-Pacific were reviewed in the discussion of merger companies in Part 1. In Fall 1995, the *United & Babson Investment Report* saw Emerson Electric outperforming many of its peers and earning at least $4.60 per share in 1996. It recommended purchasing the stock for appreciation. In its research report United & Babson also noted strong demand for Georgia-Pacific's key paper grades and potential 1996 earnings in the $14.00-$15.00 per share range.

In your quest to find stock split candidates don't ignore the industry and company fundamentals which ultimately are the driving force behind company revenues, earnings and the firm's stock market price. Look for confirmation of economic and industry trends that bode well for the company's future operations and financial performance.

The degree of management and other insider ownership signals the impact of company results on their personal wealth. Investigate how much of the firm's stock is owned by insiders and track purchases and sales by insiders. A high level of inside ownership and insider buying activity add an extra degree of assurance that management and other insiders believe in the firm's ability to earn higher earnings and deliver superior shareholder returns. Insider sales analysis can take into account the number of inside trades, the percentage of holdings purchased or sold, the number of company officers buying or selling, follow-up purchases or sales and insider reversals.

Inside sales usually contain less predictive power since many factors completely unrelated to the fundamentals of the firm can enter into the sales decision. For example, cash needed for education expenses or a new home purchase may trigger a sale of company stock by insiders.

Historically, insiders tend to be net sellers, selling around 2.3 shares for every one they purchase. Therefore, heavy insider buying is a good indication of better days ahead. H. Nejat Seyhun of the University of Michigan conducted one of the most comprehensive insider trading research studies. Seyhun concluded that insider trading can be a fairly active predictor of future stock prices and following inside trading patterns represents an effective way to earn above average returns.

One insider trading indicator uses a ratio of insider purchases to insider sales. When the ratio rises above a certain point, it is considered bullish and vice versa. While insider indicator ratios may not pinpoint the exact time to buy or sell, they can provide useful information in the overall trend of insider transactions and whether or not it is bullish or bearish for a particular stock. It's another tool in your investment kit for helping to uncover superior investment opportunities.

Insider trading information is regularly published in Standard & Poor's *The Outlook, Value Line Selection & Opinion, The Wall Street Journal,*

Barron's and *Vicker's Weekly Insider Report*. The institute for Econometric Research publishes *The Insider* which features ratings on companies with insider trades, insider market indicators, and insider buy favorites. An annual subscription costs $49. *The Insider* can be contacted at 3471 North Federal, Fort Lauderdale, Florida 33306 or call 800-442-9000.

Stock Split Prospects

This section reviews a number of companies with a history of stock splits and how the market has reacted to that news and their prospects for the future. Use them as guides for your own stock split investment analysis and tools for earning superior investment returns.

AMERICAN INTERNATIONAL GROUP

American International Group has a long history of stock dividends and stock splits, the most recent a 3-for-2 split in mid 1995. Since then the company has completed its tenth year of record earnings and its stock price continued its upward trend, recently trading in the mid-$90 per share range. Refer to Part 1 for a more in-depth look at AIG.

BED BATH & BEYOND INC.

715 Morris Avenue
Springfield, NJ 07081
201-379-1520
NASDAQ: BBBY
S & P Rating: NR

Company Profile. Bed Bath & Beyond Inc. markets a broad variety of name brand domestics and home furnishings ranging from bed linens to cookware. It operates 85 stores in over 20 states. Most of its outlets are superstores with in excess of 40,000 square-feet.

153

Financial Statistics
($ millions except per share and ratio data)

| | Fiscal Years Ending February 28 | | |
	1993	1994	1995 Est.
Working capital	54	72	100
Revenues	306	440	590
Net income(loss)	22	30	38
Long-term debt	13	17	20
Per share data	1993	1994	1995
Earnings(loss)/share	.64	.87	1.14
Dividends/share	—	—	—
Selected ratios	1993	1994	1995
Percent earned net worth	28.3	27.6	25.5
Net profit margin	7.2	6.8	6.5
Stock price range/share	1993	1994	1995
High	35 1/2	34 1/2	39 5/8
Low	13	22 7/8	18

Company Strengths. In contrast to the overall retail environment, Bed Bath & Beyond is recording strong same store sales. For the fiscal year ended February 28, 1996 net income rose 32 percent to $1.14 per share.

Investment Analysis. Bed Bath & Beyond stands to post higher earnings again in 1996 and 1997 based on anticipated store openings which are picking up speed. In addition, the company plans to garner more market share by invading new territory with forays into one or two new states in the next year. After coming to market in 1992 the firm split its stock 2-for-1 in 1993 and announced another 2-for-1 split for 1996. Look for the good times to continue unabated with earnings per share over $1.40 per share in fiscal 1996.

CLAIRE'S STORES, INC.

3 S.W. 129th Avenue
Pembroke Pines, FL 33027
305-433-3900
NYSE: CLE
S & P Rating: A-

Company Profile. Another company countering poor retail prospects, Claire's Stores, Inc. posted a strong rebound in 1995. The firm is the country's largest costume jewelry and women's accessories retailers operating over 1,000 outlets in 49 states, Canada, the Caribbean and Japan.

Financial Statistics
($ million except per share and ratio data)

| | Fiscal Years Ending February 3 | | |
	1993	1994	1995 Est.
Working capital	42	49	55
Revenues	282	301	345
Net income(loss)	24	24	30
Long-term debt	6	3	—
Per share data	1993	1994	1995
Earnings(loss)/share	.77	.77	.99
Dividends/share	.07	.08	.08
Selected ratios	1993	1994	1995
Percent earned net worth	23.7	19.5	20.0
Net profit margin	23.6	23.9	30.0
Stock price range/share	1993	1994	1995
High	13	15 3/8	15 1/4
Low	8	6 1/4	7 1/2

Company Strengths. Impressive same store sales increases rejuvenated Claire's Stores in 1995. The firm increased market penetration with the late January 1996 acquisition of 85 stores formerly operated by The Icing, Inc. Claire's has plenty of working capital and little long-term debt. It is well-positioned to capture additional market share through acquisitions and internal growth.

Investment Assessment. On top of splitting the stock in February 1996 on a 3-for-2 basis, Claire's Stores' board of directors voted a 50 percent cash stock dividend increase. New marketing thrusts targeting the teenage segment and improved margins will help boost revenues and earnings in the years ahead. The stock hit a new high of $26 per share following its stock split.

DEERE & COMPANY

**John Deere Road
Moline, IL 61265
309-765-8000
NYSE: DE
S & P Rating: B**

Company Profile. Deere & Company represents a classic turnaround company besides one with a recent stock split. After minimal earnings in fiscal 1992, the company has made steady progress on the revenues and earnings front. Deere ranks as the world's largest manufacturer of farm equipment and also manufactures and markets construction equipment, lawn and garden tractors and outdoor power equipment.

Financial Statistics
($ million except per share and ratio data)

| | Fiscal Years Ending October 31 | | |
	1993	1994	1995
Working capital	1733	2154	2212
Revenues	6479	7663	8830
Net income(loss)	168	604	706
Long-term debt	1069	1019	703
Per share data	1993	1994	1995
Earnings(loss)/share	.73	2.34	2.71
Dividends/share	.67	.68	.75

156

Selected data	1993	1994	1995
Percent earned net worth	8.1	23.6	22.9
Net profit margin	2.6	7.9	8.0

Stock price range/share	1993	1994	1995
High	26 1/8	30 1/4	38
Low	14 1/8	20 3/8	31 3/4

Company Strengths. A worldwide network of manufacturing facilities and dealers provides diversification against regional economic recessions. Likewise, the company's diversified product line helps temper a slowdown in any one product or market segment.

Investment Assessment. Deere's rebound is plowing new ground. For the first three months of fiscal 1996 ended January 31, 1996 Deere earned 63 cents per share versus only 53 cents per share for fiscal 1995's first quarter, a nearly 19 percent improvement. The board of directors voted a 3-for-1 split in November 1995 after Deere's stock had risen above $90 per share from a low of $36 per share in 1992 on a pre-split basis. It also boosted the cash dividend 9 percent. Barring any dramatic economic contraction Deere should continue to prosper.

MATTEL, INC.

333 Continental Boulevard
El Segundo, CA 90245
213-524-2000
NYSE: MAT
S & P Rating: B

Company Profile. Mattel, Inc. is the nation's largest toy maker with popular lines such as Barbie, Hot Wheels and Fisher-Price. Management has been actively pursuing acquisitions. The company operates on an international scale with over 30 percent of operating profits deriving from foreign sales.

Financial Statistics
($ million except per share and ratio data)

	1993	1994	1995
Working capital	688	627	843
Revenues	2704	3205	3639
Net income(loss)	235	303	358
Long-term debt	328	355	481
Per share data	1993	1994	1995
Earnings(loss)/share	.86	1.06	1.26
Dividends/share	.12	.15	.18
Selected ratios	1993	1994	1995
Percent earned net worth	28.8	27.9	28.1
Net profit margin	8.7	9.4	9.8
Stock price range/share	1993	1994	1995
High	15 3/4	18 7/8	24 7/8
Low	10 1/2	13 1/4	15 3/4

Company Strengths. Mattel is moving on from the failed attempt at a $5.2 billion merger with Hasbro Inc. and looking at other lucrative acquisitions. Over the past 8 years, management has successfully completed 10 acquisitions which helped the firm generate compounded annual growth rates of 20 percent and 38 percent for revenues and operating income, respectively.

Investment Assessment. Improving margins combined with key acquisitions to fill in product line gaps will deliver record earnings in 1996 and for the foreseeable future. In February, Mattel split its stock 5-for-4, the fifth stock split in less than four years. Despite disappointment over the collapse of the Hasbro deal, the market has bid up Mattel's stock price to a high of $27 1/4 per share. With double digit earnings increases projected for 1996 and 1997, the stock looks cheap. Buy for long-term appreciation.

RPM, INC.

2628 Pearl Road
P.O. Box 777
Medina, OH 44258
330-273-5090
NASDAQ: RPOW
S & P Rating: A+

Company Profile. I have followed RPM for over a decade and it has never failed to deliver consistent revenue and earnings gains via internal growth and strategic acquisitions. RPM is a diversified manufacturer of specialty chemicals, protective coatings as well servings the hobby, do-it-yourself and industrial market on a global scale.

Financial Statistics
($ million except per share and ratio data)

| | *Fiscal Years Ending May 31* | | |
	1993	*1994*	*1995*
Working capital	163	227	270
Revenues	626	816	1017
Net Income(loss)	39	53	61
Long-term debt	221	233	406
Per share data	1993	1994	1995
Earnings(loss)/share	.63	.71	.81
Dividends/share	.36	.39	.42
Selected ratios	1993	1994	1995
Percent earned net worth	16.5	16.7	17.6
Net profit margin	6.3	6.5	6.0
Stock price range/share	1993	1994	1995
High	15 1/2	15 3/4	17 1/4
Low	13	13	14 1/8

Company Strengths. A balance between coatings and specialty chemicals (55% of revenues) and consumer products (45% of revenues) provides a well-diversified income stream. RPM is a master at discovering good acquisitions and successfully building on their strengths and market niches. RPM has split its stock five times and issued a 25 percent stock dividend since late 1983. A look at the company's stock chart shows a nearly uninterrupted price rise over that time frame.

Investment Assessment. The Rust-Oleum acquisition enhances margins and RPM will stick to its pattern of generating 50 percent of revenue growth via key acquisitions. Patient shareholders have plenty of reason to be happy. The company has increased its cash dividend for 22 consecutive years. A purchase of 1,000 shares of RPM stock at $10 per share 20 years ago would be worth in excess of $800,000 today. RPM is working hard to achieve its 49th consecutive year of record revenues, earnings and earnings per share. The smart money is on RPM to succeed and higher stock prices will follow as a result. The stock is trading near the lower end of its 52-week price range. Purchase for superior investment returns.

Do Your Homework

Stock splits cannot promise higher stock prices ahead. When Texas Instruments Inc. (NYSE: TXN) splits its stock 2-for-1 in 1995 the company had enjoyed a doubling of its stock price in less than a year and was on the verge of record earnings more than 47 percent higher the record results of a year earlier. However, a royalty dispute and concerns over the declining rate of growth in the chip industry put the brakes on Texas Instruments' stock price. The stock plummeted form a post-split high of $83 1/2 per share in late 1995 to trade around $51 per share in early April 1996. The lesson is clear, do your homework on the company, economy and the industry before investing.

Even the most closely followed investors, Warren Buffet, has taken the stock split route. In a move that shocked most market pundits, Buffet's Berkshire Hathaway Inc. (NYSE: BRK) announced a plan to create unit trust shares at 1/30 of the A shares which currently sell for $33,850 per share and had a 52-week high of $38,000 per share. One drawback, the unit shares would only have voting rights 1/200 of those of the A shares. That drawback is tempered by the fact that Berkshire Hathaway has delivered an average annual return of nearly 28 percent since 1965.

Overall, stock split companies offer the chance to earn substantially higher investment returns. You owe it to yourself to investigate this unique invitation to beat the market soundly.

D
Stock
Buybacks

Record Stock Buybacks

Corporations repurchased their common stock at record rates during 1994 and 1995. According to the Securities Data Company in Newark, New Jersey announced stock buyback transactions in 1995 totaled more than $98 billion, eclipsing the previous record of $69.3 million set only a year earlier.

Among the largest announced stock repurchases in 1995 was E.I. duPont de Nemours & Company's decision to buyback 156 million or 23 percent of its outstanding common shares via a privately negotiated buyback valued at $8.3 billion. The transaction also carried major merger implications as The Seagram Company Ltd used the proceeds of the sale of its DuPont holdings to finance the purchase of an 80 percent interest in MCA Inc. and paydown long-term debt. The DuPont deal overshadowed the $5 billion stock repurchase program announced by General Electric Company in 1994.

Financial institutions also entered the stock buyback arena in full force. Wells Fargo & Company amended a previously announced buyback program to allow for the purchase of up to $3 billion of its common stock in open market transactions. The nation's largest banking company, Citicorp, also got into the act with the expansion of its repurchase program to buy back another $3 billion in common stock and convertible preferred shares over the next two years. American Express Company also plans to buy

163

back up to 40 million of its common shares, approximately 8 percent of the total outstanding, for a value around $1.4 billion.

On the pharmaceutical front, Merck & Company announced its intent to repurchase up to $3 billion of its common stock in both open market transactions and privately negotiated deals. Other industries joined in the stock buyback activity. For example, in 1995 chemical giant Union Carbide Corporation's board of directors authorized the repurchase of 10 million shares equaling 7.1 percent of its outstanding common stock. In June 1995 construction and earth moving equipment maker Caterpillar Inc. boosted its dividend 40 percent and announced its intention to repurchase as much as $200 million or 10 percent of its outstanding shares over the next three to five years. Publisher Harcourt General, Inc. moved to authorize the repurchase of up to 2.5 million shares of its common stock, copper producer Phelps Dodge Corporation's board of directors approved the buyback of up to 5 million of its nearly 71 million outstanding shares and Kerr McGee Corporation used part of the proceeds from the sale of refining and marketing assets to declare an 8 percent increase in its cash dividend and repurchase as much as $300 million in common stock. Overall, there were more than 1,100 stock buyback programs in effect in the United States during 1995.

The pace of stock buybacks has been carried into 1996. Stock purchase programs have been expanded or initiated by a variety of companies in the full range of industries. During the first quarter of 1996 BankAmerica Corporation adopted a new share repurchase plan to buy up to $2 billion of its common stock by the end of 1997; newsprint producer Bowater Inc. raised its cash dividend by 33 percent and said it plans to buy back up to 10 percent of its outstanding common stock; Federal Home Loan Mortgage Corporation (Freddie Mac) announced a buy back program to acquire as much as $1 billion of its stock; and chemical and biotechnology firm Monsanto Company used an interesting combination to increase and decrease its outstanding shares with a proposed 4-to-1 or 5-to-1 stock split in conjunction with a resumed stock repurchase plan designed to buy as many as 8 million shares.

164

Why Companies Repurchase Their Shares

Companies buy back their stock for a variety of reasons. First of all, a stock repurchase program can be initiated to thwart a takeover bid. Reducing the number of outstanding shares boosts the value of those remaining while decreasing corporate cash reserves which often attract raiders.

Stock purchases can lead to improved cash flow in the long run. While the outlay to repurchase stock may reduce available cash reserves, the company conserves cash in the long-term by reducing its cash dividend payments.

Stock buybacks also work to improve the operating performance of the company. Shrinking the equity base boosts earnings per share and return on equity performance numbers. This enhancement of shareholder return can be given an additional upward jolt with the simultaneous announcement of a hike in the cash dividend. At the same time, stock buybacks work to shore up and bolster the company's stock market price. With fewer shares outstanding the demand for a company's stock, as investors chase fewer shares, can drive prices higher or at least provide support against price declines. As mentioned above, better per share performance numbers and enhanced return on equity are viewed favorably by investors, creating more demand for the stock and raising its price.

Stock buybacks and the resulting increased performance comparisons represent a significant psychological boost and the market reacts to psychological factors. Financial analysts favor stocks exhibiting improving earnings per share and return on equity. Repurchase programs enchance these period-to-period comparisons. This can result in initial research analyst recommendations and upgrades which can translate into higher stock prices and increased price/earnings multiples.

Performance can also be enhanced with the reduction in the number of shareholders. The administrative cost of servicing the shareholder base can be substantial. The expense of corporate shareholder department personnel, annual report expenses, trust services, dividend payments, SEC reporting requirements, press releases and other shareholders communications are all related to the size of the shareholder base. These rising costs can impact a company's decision to repurchase stock.

Companies may also repurchase shares for reasons not directly related to their performance numbers or attempts to reduce the number of shares outstanding. To illustrate, Microsoft Corporation bought back $698 million or 11.7 million of its shares over a 12-month period in order to have shares available to distribute to its employees exercising stock options. In this case, after all repurchased shares are reissued to employees, there has been no lasting change in the amount of shares outstanding and any impact on earnings per share and return on equity are a temporary illusion.

Companies may also repurchase shares to accomodate companies closely associated with the repurchasing corporation. The DuPont/ Seagram deal represents such a situation. Seagram needed capital to move ahead with its move on MCA. DuPont came through. Likewise, a large shareholder or retiring officer or director may desire to dispose of a large block of company shares through a negotiated repurchase by the company.

Joint venture partners may also obtain shares of their contemporaries or larger firms may receive shares of smaller companies in exchange for helping to fund research and product development efforts. Formal repurchase agreements may be entered into at the onset of the partnership or they may result as the outcome of changes in the partnership relationship.

Other reasons for corporations to have readily issuable shares on hand include using them to acquire other companies in exchange for stock or combinations of cash and stock or for other forms of employees plans such as stock bonuses, ESOPs (Employee Stock Ownership Plans) and dividend reinvestment plans.

Perhaps one of the best reasons for a company to repurchase its own stock is as an investment. Simply put it may be the best use and offer the best return for its cash. Investing in its own shares may provide a better return than making pricey acquisitions, research or development or spending for additional production facilities which may result in overcapacity. Management may consider the company undervalued at its current stock price and move to capitalize when the company's stock price rises.

Charles Neuhauser, senior vice president with Investment Counselors of Maryland in Baltimore, recounts the story of a company which hired a consulting firm to seek out the best acquisition candidate. The advisor came back with the recommendation of an investment which far surpassed any others analyzed in return on investment. When management asked the name of the potential acquisition the advisor replied, "Purchase your own company's stock."

The stock repurchase may take several forms. Companies can buy back their stock in the open market, negotiate private purchases with large shareholders and/or initiate a tender offer to purchase shares directly from share-holders.

Open market purchases are carried out under programs authorized by the board of directors and represent the most prevalent method of buying back stock. They are executed through a broker/dealer within specific purchase guidelines or limits set by the company. Limits may include reference to percentage of transactions occurring on the exchange, purchasing at the open or close of daily trading and up-tick restrictions. Most tender orders are for a minimum number of shares and for a specific period of time. The tender offer typically offers to repurchase the shares at a premium over the prevailing market price.

Stock Buyback Research

According to a study presented at the 1994 National Bureau of Economic Research Behavorial Finance meeting and published in the *Journal of Financial Economics*, covering the years 1980 through 1990, the stock prices of 1,239 companies announcing stock buybacks moved well ahead of the market immediately after the stock repurchase news was released. More importantly, for the 36 months following the buyback announcement, stock prices of these companies on average outperformed the general market by approximately 13 percent. Furthermore, if the buyback company stocks were in the "value" category, they beat the market by about 45 percent over the subsequent 48 months.

According to the study prepared by David Ikenberry of Rice University's Jesse H. Jones Graduate School of Administration in Houston, Josef Lakonishok of the University of Illinois at Urbana-Champaign and Theo Vermaelen from the French institute INSEAD and the University of Limburg, the average buyback stock rose 3.5 percent on the day of the announcement, with small caps leading the pack. The sample included 1,239 open market share repurchases announced between January 1980 and December 1990 by firms whose shares traded on the New York Stock Exchange, American Stock Exchange or NASDAQ.

As indicated above, the market outperformance by buyback stocks continued through four years after the announcement. Compared with a benchmark portfolio representing the general market, a buy-and-hold portfolio of buyback stocks outperformed the market by 12.1 percent over the four year period following the buyback pronouncement.

Within the composite outperformance lurk some interesting statistics. For example, value stocks outperformed the market by 45.3 percent during the four year time frame with a compound return of 88.62 percent. The research team defined value stocks as the 20 percent of the repurchase stock sample with the highest book-to-market ratios. For repurchases announced by "glamour" stocks, where undervaluation is less likely to be an important motive, the researchers found no positive drift in abnormal returns.

The research study concluded that stock buyback programs can be important indicators to investors. This is particularly true when the repurchased stocks are already selling at low price-to-book or price-to-earnings ratios.

Consistent with prior research, larger repurchase programs are received more favorably by the market. For example, programs which purchase more than 10 percent of outstanding shares delivered a positive abnormal return of 4.51 percent versus an abnormal positive return of 2.58 percent for repurchase programs for less than 2.5 percent of the outstanding shares.

Takeover activity also comes into play in the stock repurchase scenario. A high incidence of these firms are subject to takeovers and suitors can influence their stock prices. Still, the three-year compounded abnormal return for the surviors came in at 6.7 percent compared with 13.0 percent for a sample of firms which survived at least four years following the buyback announcement.

Another of the most important research findings for individual investors is the fact that the information conveyed by open market share repurchases is largely ignored by the market. These market inefficiencies and trends open up opportunities for alert investors to earn investment gains that far surpass those delivered by the overall market.

Ford Investors Services, Inc. in San Diego, California issued an October 31, 1995 Share Buyback Indicator Special Study Report. According to Tim Alward, director of marketing, the buyback analysis measured the performance from the month of the actual repurchase of shares rather than using the announcement date since some companies do not carry through on their announced repurchase plans.

The Ford Investor Services study reflected that any company repurchasing one percent or more shares outperformed the Ford database universe. The higher the buyback the better the stock performance of the buyback company. The results held true for the 5-year, 10-year and 20-year time frames. For example, the Ford Universe earned an average annual return of 19.2 percent for the period December 1974 through December 1994. During the same time frame, companies that repurchased between 1 percent to 5 percent of their stock earned 23.7 percent while companies that repurchased between 5 percent and 10 percent earned 26.6 percent and firms buying back over 10 percent of their outstanding stock earned 28.8 percent. As illustrated in Chart 2-4 similar results occurred in the five and ten year periods.

Average Annual Returns
Stock Buyback Companies Versus Universe

| Period | Shares Repurchased | | | |
	10% or more	5% to 10%	1% to 5%	Universe
12/74-12/94	28.8	26.6	23.7	19.2
12/84-12/94	19.8	20.3	19.0	14.4
12/89-12/94	18.3	18.3	13.5	10.8

Chart 2-4 Data courtesy of Ford Investor Services, Inc.

Be aware that stock repurchase programs are authorizations by the board of directors for the company to buyback shares, however, they are not firm commitments to complete or even initiate the shares repurchases. Birinyi Associates, a research firm in Greenwich, Connecticut, estimates that on average corporations follow through on only 20 percent of the stock repurchase programs they announce.

No matter how you slice it, it makes good sense to pay attention to announced stock repurchase programs. Analyze the companies behind the stock buybacks, take into account the size of the buyback, discern if the stock will be retired or reissued under employee benefit plans or other purposes, try to decipher management's real intent and whether or not the company is likely to make the share repurchases and evaluate the company to see if the stock repurchase announcement is a signal that the company is truly undervalued.

Divining Buyback Candidates

Of course you can wait for companies to announce their intentions before you begin your stock buyback research. However, you can improve on the already impressive investment gains promised by stock buyback companies with a little upfront analysis and investing in the companies prior to their share repurchase program pronouncement.

Here's how to ferret out prospective buyback companies and beat other investors to the punch. Use research sources such as *Moody's Handbook of Common Stocks*, *Moody's Handbook of Nasdaq Stocks*, Standard & Poor's tear sheets and the *Value Line Investment Survey* to assist in your analysis. If you are computer savvy a number of stock analysis programs are available that allow you to screen stocks based on a number of variables and key ratios.

— Naturally, companies that have established and acted on stock repurchase programs in the past are likely to embark on new or additional buyback programs. This is especially true if the company's stock price reacted with above average performance following completion of the purchases. Review the stock price charts of firms with a prior history of completing stock buybacks.

— Search out companies with large cash positions and strong cash flows. These 'cash cows' are tempting targets for potential corporate raiders and management may take action to reduce their cash position and enhance shareholder value. In the same vein companies with corporate coffers full of cash may determine that the best place to invest the excess capital is their own stock. As mergers and acquisitions heat up and the prices of deals start to skyrocket this may force management to forgo the acquisition route and turn toward investing in the company's own shares. Analyzing the firm's Statement of Cash Flows will show if the company is generating excess cash. The *Value Line Investment Survey* includes a listing of the Biggest 'Free Flow' Cash Generators.

— Uncovering undervalued situations can also lead you to potential stock purchase companies. Look for firms whose stock market value is low in comparison with its underlying book value and research analyst estimates. Value Line and other financial publications routinely list companies which are undervalued as determined by wide discounts from book value, low price/earnings ratio, low price to net working capital ratio, low debt-equity ratio and other yardsticks.

Buyback Beauties

The following companies deserve a close look as companies engaged in share buyback programs which could help deliver superior investment returns over the long-term.

BANKAMERICA CORPORATION

NYSE: BAC
S & P Rating: B

In March 1996 BankAmerica Corporation adpoted a new share repurchase plan designed to buy back up to $2 billion of the bank's common shares (approximately 7 percent) and $1 billion of its preferred stock. A rebounding California economy, growing international business and a heavy thrust into private banking bode well for BankAmerica.

BIOMET, INC.

NASDAQ: BMET
S & P Rating: B+

Biomet, Inc. comes to attention for several reasons. First of all, it is is a large free flow cash generator. Second, it has a long- term track record of solid earnings increases. Third, the company has a history of splitting its stock. Finally, negative publicity on a patent infringment suit and product competition drove down the firm's stock price 30 percent to the $14 per share level. In light of the company's long-term prospects the sharp price drop is an overreaction. The company could take advantage of the situation and use its strong cash flow to repurchase shares and boost earnings comparisons and return on equity.

COMMERCIAL METALS COMPANY

NYSE: CMC
S & P Rating: B+

Commercial Metals authorized the purchase of up to 500,000 (3.3 percent) of its outstanding common shares in January 1996. A return to a more robust economy will boost industrial and commercial construction and demand for the company's steel products and fabrication services.

DOW CHEMICAL COMPANY

NYSE: DOW
S & P Rating: B

In mid-1995 Dow Chemical launched a stock buyback program to reacquire 25 million (9 percent) of its common shares. Dow has plenty of cash from the Marion Merrell Dow sale to expand the program. Look for continued earnings gains. With the stock trading near $85 per share Dow ranks as a stock split candidate as well.

FEDERAL HOME LOAN MORTGAGE CORPORATION

NYSE: FRE
S & P Rating: NR

The Federal Home Loan Mortgage Corporation, popularly known as Freddie Mac, board of directors authorized the repurchase of as much as $1 billion of its stock. The company recently finished a $200 million buyback and the March 1996 new authorization allows the purchase of an additional 12 million shares (12 percent) of outstanding stock. The board also increased its quarterly cash dividend by nearly 17 percent.

   Both Freddie Mac and Fannie Mae below were recommended as attractive investments for 1996 by David Dreman, author of *Contrarian Investment Strategy* and chairman and chief executive officer of Dreman Value

Management, on CNBC during April 1996. Dreman cited both companies for their long-term records of growth rates around 15 percent.

FEDERAL NATIONAL MORTGAGE ASSOCIATION

NYSE: FNM
S & P Rating: A-

Interest rate worries aside, Fannie Mae is well-positioned to perform well in the months and years ahead. In January 1996 the company moved to repurchase as much of 6 percent of its outstanding shares and also enacted a 4-for-1 stock split.

FIRST BANK SYSTEM, INC.

NYSE: FBS
S & P Rating: B-

Recovering from its failed attempt to acquire First Interstate Bancorp, First Bank System is putting its huge cash arsenal to use repurchasing its own stock. The bank holding company aggressively expanded a share-repurchase program in February 1996 to buy up to 25 million (17 percent) common shares by the end of 1997. At the same time the board of directors raised the cash dividend 14 percent.

FOREST CITY ENTERPRISES INC.

AMEX: FCEA, FCEB
S & P Rating: NR

On the heels of a record year, Forest City Enterprises' board of directors authorized a repurchase plan to buy back up to 250,000 shares of the company's Class A and Class B common shares on the open market. The real estate management and development firm stands to gain from its budding financial services segment and forays into fast growing real estate markets such as Las Vegas.

GENERAL ELECTRIC COMPANY

NYSE: GE
S & P Rating: A+

Bill Staton considers General Electric Company a classic buyback situation. The company is in the midst of a major stock repurchase program with $3 billion in shares already purchased and another $6 billion yet to be acquired. General Electric ranks as one of Staton's "America's Finest Companies." General Electric has delivered 19 years of higher earnings and dividends and paid cash dividends every year since 1899. Double digit earnings gains are backed by strong international market expansion, a full new product pipeline and a renewed thrust in its finance and service segments. In addition to the ongoing stock reduction program, General Electric has split its stock 2-for-1 twice in the past decade.

LOGICON, INC.

NYSE: LGN
S & P Rating: A

Logicon, Inc. operates in the consolidating defense industry and its large free flow cash generating position could make it an attractive takeover target. Therefore, the company may decide to repurchase shares as a defensive measure. Logicon stock draws attention for several other reasons. Steadily improving earnings are bolstered by niche military electronic and training product and service segments. A takeover bid could drive up its stock price or a share repurchase program could enhance earnings comparisons. In addition, the company has split its stock twice in four years.

MERCK & COMPANY

NYSE: MRK
S & P Rating: A+

Merck closed out 1995 with a 13 percent gain in earnings per share and over $1.8 billion in cash and cash equivalents. Tremendous new product potential, strong finances and expanding international business opportunities make Merck a strong long-term holding for superior investment performance. Merck could take action to split its stock or repurchase its shares and bears watching.

REYNOLDS & REYNOLDS COMPANY

NYSE: REY
S & P Rating: B+

Business forms producer and computer systems provider Reynolds & Reynolds has been on a roll with earnings per share growth in excess of 20 percent for several years running. I included Reynolds & Reynolds in my book, *The 105 Best Investments for the 21st Century* (McGraw-Hill, 1995). Since then the company stock has consistently hit new highs and now trades above $51 per share, rising 57 percent above its 52-week low. Over the past three years, the company has repurchased over 3 million of its common shares and a 1995 extension of its buyback program will increase that total to nearly 6 million shares. As of early 1996 there were 41 million shares outstanding. The company split its stock 2-for-1 in early 1994 and could take that action once again should the stock price rise another 20 percent.

A. SCHULMAN INC.

NASDAQ: SHLM
S & P Rating: A

A. Schulman Inc.'s shares dropped nearly 20 percent after the company reported fiscal fourth quarter earnings below expectations due to a drop in pricing for the firm's specialty resins. The bad news extended into the first quarter of fiscal 1996 with an earnings per share decline of nearly 35 percent. As a result Schulman's stock trades around $23 per share, 35 percent below its 52-week high of $32 3/4 per share.

All of this makes Schulman interesting from several vantage points. The company has a long history stock splits, the most recent a 5-for-4 split in early 1994. A rebounding ecomony promises to boost prices of basic raw materials and could boost demand for Shulman's products and earnings per share, making the company an enticing turnaround prospect. Finally, in November 1995 the board of directors confirmed a stock repurchase authorization first made in 1987 to buy back up to 4 million of the company's common shares. Feeling that its shares are now undervalued, the company has finally made its initial repurchases under the 1987 authorization.

STANDEX INTERNATIONAL CORPORATION

NYSE: SXI
S & P Rating: A

Standex International is one of those market anomalies. As noted in Part 1, many conglomerates are finding ways to split themselves into several new companies or spinning off subsidiaries or operating segments into new entities. Standex International, on the other hand, goes on its merry way acquiring a myriad of businesses in a variety of industries.

While earnings gains in fiscal 1996 look to be modest, Standex will still earn above average return on net worth partially as a result of its aggressive stock repurchase program. Since the initiation of its stock buyback program in 1985, the company has retired nearly 18 million shares comprising more than half of its outstanding stock. It recently expanded the share repurchase program to acquire another 1 million shares. In January 1996 a million share block of Standex stock changed hands as the stock price dropped as low as $26 1/8 per share. Of that total Standex repurchased 193,000 shares.

176

UNIFORCE TEMPORARY PERSONNEL, INC.

NASDAQ: UNFR
S & P Rating: NR

Uniforce Temporary Personnel made a tender offer for 30 percent of its outstanding shares through January 10, 1996 at $11 1/4 per share. The company recognized an undervalued situation and took action. Since then Uniforce's stock price hit a new high of $30 3/4 per share in the first half of 1996. Uniforce operates in the highly fragmented but consolidating temporary industry. Earnings have been on a steady upward slope, jumping more than 27 percent in 1995. You can purchase Uniforce for its takeover possibilites, strong growth potential, as a potential stock buyback company or as a stock split candidate. Under any of the above scenarios Uniforce looks like an investment that can deliver superior returns over the long-term.

It's time for you to join the pros on Wall Street and make megabucks on mergers and these other unique investment opportunities. Good luck.

The author of
INVESTOR'S GUIDE FOR MAKING MEGABUCKS ON MERGERS
invites you to examine these special offers:

The Hometown Investor   Learn how to find investment treasures in your back yard; covers everything from stocks to municipal bonds to IPOS

105 Best Inv. for the 21st Century   Find out which companies are well-positioned to outperform in the 21st century; highlights the best of the best stocks, mutual funds, ADRs and other investments for various economic scenarios.

Divining the Dow   Study the collection of 100 of the world's most widely followed stock market prediction systems; includes economic, technical, stock and market indicators such as the Elliott Wave, Barron's Confidence Index, and Earnings Revision Effect.

Main Street Beats Wall Street   Follow the profiles of five successful investment clubs; explains how and why investment clubs outperform the professionals on Wall Street, analyzes top investment club stocks that promise to outperform the market.

Money Making Investments   Diversify your portfolio, reduce risk and enhance performance with American Depositary Receipts (ADRS), convertibles, preferreds, zero coupon bonds and warrants; presents unique investment opportunities your broker doesn't tell you about.

Stock Picking   Use corporate cashflow to pick star performers and ferret out small-cap gems and value situations; gives the 11 best tactics for beating the market, proven techniques used by Wall Street's elite such as John Templeton and David Dreman.

Wall Street Words   Keep this guide to the terminology of Wall Street as a handy reference; includes as a bonus information on basic trading strategies and fundamental and technical analysis.

> *"...a useful reference to clarify the meaning of hundreds of new specialized words often used by investors."*

Sir John Templeton, Chairman Templeton Funds

Utility & Energy Portfolio (quarterly)   Covers the changing utility and energy industry; EVERY BUY/SELL RECOMMENDATION A WINNER SINCE INCEPTION OF NEWSLETTER IN 1992; WorldCom up 60%, Southwest Energy up 30%, Cincinnati Bell Up 25%

178

21st Century Investments (quarterly) Provides regular updates on investments in "The 105 Best Investments for the 21st Century" and other stocks poised to outperform into the next century; Danka Business Systems up 50%, St. Jude Medical up 40%, Reynolds & Reynolds up 36%.

Gaming & Investments Quarterly Ferrets out unique investments in the explosive gaming, recreation, leisure industry; Caesars World 34% gain, Caesars World short sale 21% gain, Casino America 42% gain, Sodak Gaming 74% gain.

— — — — — — — — — — Tear Here — — — — — — — — — —

NAME _____ SIGNATURE _____

ADDRESS _____

CITY/STATE/ZIP _____

DISCOVER CARD # _____

EXP DATE _____

OR SEND CHECK OR MONEY ORDER TO: 21st CENTURY PUBLISHERS
1320 CURT GOWDY DRIVE
CHEYENNE, WY 82009

Yes, I want to improve my investment performance. Please send the following COMMON SENSE INVESTMENT GUIDES.

BONUS OFFERS: (1) FREE ANNUAL SUBSCRIPTION to newsletter (Circle choice) with order of three books. (2) FREE PORTFOLIO ANALYSIS with any paid order of $60 or more (up to three common stocks). (3) FREE COPY OF "WALL STREET WORDS" with paid subscription to *Utility & Energy Portfolio*.

INVESTMENT BOOKS	SPECIAL PRICE
Hometown Investor ($22.95)	$ 20.00
105 Best Inv. for 21st Century ($22.95)	20.00
Divining the Dow ($24.95)	21.00
Main Street Beats Wall Street ($22.95)	20.00
Money Making Investments ($22.95)	20.00
Stock Picking ($14.95)	12.00
Wall Street Words ($14.95)	12.00
NEWSLETTERS	
Utility & Energy Portfolio ($95/yr)	35.00
21st Century Inv. ($95/yr) intro price	15.00
Gaming & Investments Quarterly ($75/yr)	25.00
Subtotal	$_____ . ____
Add $1.50 per book shipping (U.S. orders)	_____ . ____
Total	$_____ . ____

Glossary

ACCRETED. The process of earning or growing gradually. For example, the interest on zero coupon bonds is accreted.

ADJUSTABLE RATE PREFERRED. A preferred security with its dividend payment pegged to a specific index or indices.

AMERICAN DEPOSITARY RECEIPT (ADR). A negotiable receipt for shares of a foreign corporation held in the vault of a United States depository bank.

ANNUAL REPORT. The Securities and Exchange Commission required report presenting a portrayal of the company's operations and financial position. It includes a balance sheet, income statement, statement of cash flows, description of company operations, management discussion of company financial condition and operating results and any events which materially impact the company.

ASSET ALLOCATION. Investment strategy of reducing risk and increasing return by investing in a variety of asset types.

ASSET PLAY. A stock investment that value investors find attractive due to asset undervaluation by the market.

AT THE MONEY. The situation when the underlying security's market price equals the exercise price.

BASIS PRICE. The cost of an investment used to determine capital gains or losses.

BEAR HUG. An unsolicited acquisition offer submitted to management or the board of directors of the target company. The offer is designed to force the target to publicly disclose the offer and enter into negotiations with the bidder.

BEAR MARKET. A period of time during which stock prices decline over a period of months or years.

BOND. A long-term debt security which obligates the issuer to pay interest and repay the principal. The holder does not have any ownership rights in the issuer.

BOND RATIO. The measure of a company's leverage comparing the firm's debt to total capital.

BOTTOM UP INVESTING. Investment strategy starting with company fundamentals and then moving to the overall economic and investment environment.

BUSTED. A convertible whose underlying common stock value has fallen so low that the convertible provision no longer holds any value.

CALL OPTION. A contract providing the holder the right to buy the underlying security at a specific price during a specified time period.

CALL PROVISION. A provision allowing the security issuer to recall the security before maturity.

CASH EQUIVALENT. An asset type with maturities of less than one year.

CASH FLOW. The flow of funds in and out of an operating business. Normally calculated as net income plus depreciation and other non-cash items.

CASH FLOW/DEBT RATIO. The relationship of free cash flow to total long-term indebtedness. This ratio is helpful in tracking a firm's ability to meet scheduled debt and interest payment requirements.

CASH FLOW/INTEREST RATIO. How many times free cash flow will cover fixed interest payments on long-term debt.

CASH FLOW PER SHARE. The amount earned before deduction for depreciation and other charges not involving the outlay of cash.

CASH RATIO. Used to measure liquidity. It is calculated as the sum of cash and marketable securities divided by current liabilities. It indicates how well a company can meet current liabilities.

CLOSED-END FUND. An investment fund with a fixed number of shares outstanding and trades on exchanges like stock in regular companies.

CLUSTER INVESTING. Method of diversification recommending investing in stocks from different clusters or groups.

COLLAR. In a stock-for-stock acquisition, a provision for the adjustment of the exchange ratio in order to guarantee that the target company's shareholders will receive securities having a specified minimum market value.

COMMON and PREFERRED CASH FLOW COVERAGE RATIOS. How many times annual free cash flow will cover common and preferred cash dividend payments.

COMMON STOCK RATIO. The relationship of common stock to total company capitalization.

CONTRARIAN. An investor seeking securities out-of-favor with other investors.

CONVERTIBLE. A security that is exchangeable into common stock at the option of the holder under specified terms and conditions.

COVERED CALL. An option in which the investor owns the underlying security.

CROWN JEWEL. A company's most attractive asset or line of business.

CUMULATIVE. As it relates to preferred stock, any unpaid preferred dividends that accrue and must be paid prior to resumption of common stock dividends.

CURRENT RATIO. A liquidity ratio calculated by dividing current assets by current liabilities.

CYCLES. Repeating patterns of business, economic and market activity.

CYCLICAL. Industries and companies that advance and decline in relation to the changes in the overall economic environment.

DEBT-TO-EQUITY RATIO. The relationship of debt to shareholder's equity in a firm's capitalization structure.

DEFENSIVE INVESTMENTS. Securities that are less affected by economic contractions, thus offering downside price protection.

DEFINITIVE AGREEMENT. A legally binding agreement which explicitly sets forth the representations, obligations and rights of each party, including the conditions under which the merger can be terminated.

DIVERSIFICATION. The spreading of investment risk by owning different types of securities, investments in different geographical markets, etc.

DOLLAR COST AVERAGING. Investment strategy of investing a fixed amount of money over time to achieve a lower average security purchase price.

DOW JONES INDUSTRIAL AVERAGE. Market index consisting of 30 U.S. industrial companies. Used as a measure of market performance.

DOW THEORY. Investment theory that the market moves in three simultaneous movements, which help forecast the direction of the economy and the market.

DRIP. Dividend reinvestment plan in which stockholders can purchase additional shares with dividends and/or cash.

EARNINGS PER SHARE. Net after-tax income divided by the number of outstanding company shares.

ECONOMIC SERIES. The complete cycle of types of economic periods such as from expansion to slowdown to contraction to recession/ depression to increased activity back to expansion.

ECONOMIC VALUE. With respect to stock, the anticipated free cash flow the company will generate over a period of time, discounted by the weighted cost of a company's capital.

EFFICIENT MARKET. A market that instantly takes into account all known financial information and reflects it in the security's price.

EXCHANGE OFFER. An offer made directly to the target company's shareholders soliciting the exchange of their shares for the bidder's securities. No shareholder vote is required.

EXERCISE PRICE. The price at which an option or futures contract can be executed. Also known as the striking price.

EXPIRATION DATE. The last day on which an option or future can be exercised.

FAIRNESS LETTER. An opinion, usually written by an investment banker and addressed to the board of directors, as to the fairness of a proposed reorganization from the standpoint of the company's shareholders.

FEDERAL RESERVE. The national banking system consisting of 12 independent federal reserve banks in Atlanta, Boston, Chicago, Cleveland, Dallas, Kansas City, Minneapolis, New York, Philadelphia, Richmond, St. Louis and San Francisco.

FISCAL YEAR. The 12-month accounting period that conforms to the company's natural operating cycle versus the calendar year.

FREDDIE MAC. The nickname of the Federal Home Loan Mortgage Corporation.

FREE CASH FLOW. Determined by calculating operating earnings after taxes and then adding depreciation and other noncash expenses, less capital expenditures and increases in working capital.

FREE CASH FLOW/EARNINGS RATIO. The percentage of earnings actually available in cash. It is the percentage of free cash available to company management for investments, acquisitions, plant construction, dividends, etc.

FUNDAMENTAL ANALYSIS. Investment strategy focusing on the intrinsic value of the company as evidenced by a review of the balance sheet, income statement, cash flow, operating performance, etc.

GAP. A trading pattern when the price range from one day does not overlap the previous day's price range.

GLOBAL DEPOSITARY RECEIPT (GDR). Similar to ADR. Depositary receipt issued in the international community representing shares in a foreign company. Other designations include International Depositary Receipt (IDR) and European Depositary Receipt(EDR).

GREENMAIL. A corporate repurchase of a block of stock at a premium price in order to remove the threat of an unfriendly takeover attempt by the seller.

GROWTH INVESTMENTS. Companies or industries with earnings projected to outpace the market consistently over the long-term.

HART-SCOTT-RODINO. Legislation that requires that the parties to certain mergers provide advance notice of their plans to the Justice Department and the Federal Trade Commission and satisfy specified waiting-period requirements before consummating the merger.

HIGH-TECH STOCK. Securities of firms in high-technology industries such as biotechnology, computers, electronics, lasers, medical devices and robotics.

HYBRID SECURITY. A security that possesses the characteristics of both stock and bonds, such as a convertible bond.

INDENTURE. The legal contract spelling out the terms and conditions between the issuer and bondholders.

INDEX. Compilation of performance for specific groupings of stocks or mutual funds such as the Dow Jones Industrial Average, S & P 500, etc.

INDICATOR. A measurement of the economy or securities markets used by economists and investment analysts to predict future economic and financial moves and direction. Indicators are classified as leading, coincidental or lagging. Indicator examples include interest rate changes, utility consumption, number of unemployment claims, etc.

IPO (INITIAL PUBLIC OFFERING). The first public offering of a company's stock.

INSIDER. Anyone having access to material corporate information. Most frequently used to refer to company officers, directors and top management.

INSTITUTIONAL INVESTOR. Investor organizations, such as pension funds and money managers, who trade large volumes of securities.

IN THE MONEY. The situation when the price of the underlying security is above the exercise price.

INTRINSIC VALUE. The difference between the current market price of the underlying security and the striking price of a related option.

JUNK BOND. A bond with ratings below investment grade.

LEADING INDICATOR. An economic measurement that tends to accurately predict the future direction of the economy or stock market.

LEAPS. Long-term equity participation securities. Long-term options with maturities up to two years.

LEVERAGE. The use of debt to finance a company's operations. Also, the use of debt by investors to increase the return on investment from securities transactions.

LEVERAGED BUYOUT. A reorganization in which a group of investors, usually acting in conjunction with management, purchases control of the target company with borrowed funds that are secured by the target's assets.

LIFE CYCLE INVESTING. Developing an investment strategy based on where you are in your life cycle.

LIQUIDATION. A reorganization in which a company's assets are sold piecemeal to various buyers and the net proceeds distributed to shareholders.

LIQUIDITY. The degree of ease in which assets can be turned into readily available cash.

LISTED. Investment securities that have met the listing requirements of a particular exchange.

LOCK-UP. A provision of a merger agreement which gives the proposed bidder certain advantages over other potential acquirers.

MAINTENANCE MARGIN. The minimum equity value that must be maintained in a margin account. Initial margin requirements include a minimum deposit of $2,000 before any credit can be extended. Current Regulation T rules require maintenance margin equal at least 50 percent of the market value of the margined positions.

MARGIN. The capital (in cash or securities) that an investor deposits with a broker to borrow additional funds to purchase securities.

MARGIN CALL. A demand from a broker for additional cash or securities as collateral to bring the margin account back within maintenance limits.

MUNICIPAL BOND. A bond issued by a local or state government or government agency.

MUTUAL FUND. An investment company that sells shares in itself to the investing public and uses the proceeds to purchase individual securities.

NAFTA. North American Free Trade Agreement.

NAKED OPTION. An option written when the investor does not have a position in the underlying security.

NASDAQ. National Association of Securities Dealers Automated Quotation System, providing computerized quotes of market makers for stocks traded over the counter.

NET ASSET VALUE (NAV). The quoted market value of a mutual fund share. Determined by dividing the closing market value of all securities owned by the mutual fund plus all other assets and liabilities by the total number of shares outstanding.

OPEC. The Organization of Petroleum Exporting Countries.

OPTION. A security that gives the holder the right to purchase or sell a particular investment at a fixed price for a specified period of time.

OUT OF THE MONEY. A call option whose striking price is higher than the underlying security's current market price; a put option or whose striking price is lower than the current market price.

PARTICIPATING. As it relates to preferred stock, the preferred stockholder shares in additional dividends as the earnings of the company improve.

PAYOUT RATIO. The percentage of a company's profit paid out in cash dividends.

POISON PILL. A security issued by a target company to its shareholders which has special provisions that would make an unfriendly takeover extremely expensive for the acquirer.

PORTFOLIO. The investment holdings of an individual or institutional investor; including stocks, bonds, options, money market accounts, etc.

PREFERRED. A security with preference to dividends and claim to corporate assets over common stock.

PRICE/EARNINGS RATIO. Determined by dividing the stock's market price by its earnings per common share. Used as an indicator of company performance and in comparison with other stock investments and the overall market.

PRIVATE PLACEMENT. The placement of a security directly with a person, business, or other entity without any offering to the general investing public.

PROSPECTUS. The SEC required printed summary of the registration statement. The prospectus contains critical information about the security offering such as business, management, and financial information.

PROXY FIGHT. An attempt to gain control of a target company by voting out the existing board of directors and replacing it with a new slate supported by the insurgents, often for the purpose of pursuing a reorganization of the company.

PUT OPTION. A contract giving the holder the right to sell the underlying security at a specific price over a specified time frame.

QUICK RATIO. Current assets less inventory divided by current liabilities. Used to measure corporate liquidity, it is regarded as an improvement over the current ratio, which includes the usually not very liquid inventory.

REIT. Real Estate Investment Trust.

RAIDER. An individual or corporation with a reputation for attempting unfriendly takeovers.

RANGE. The high and low prices over which the security trades during a specific time frame—day, month, 52-weeks, etc.

RATING. Independent ranking of a security in regard to risk and ability to meet payment obligations.

REBALANCING. The process of adjusting a portfolio mix to return to a desired asset allocation level.

RELATIVE STRENGTH. Comparison of a security's earnings or stock price strength in relation to other investments or indices.

RISK. The financial uncertainty that the actual return will vary from the expected return. Risk factors include inflation, deflation, interest rate risk, market risk, liquidity, default, etc.

RULE OF EIGHT. Diversification strategy that contends a minimum of eight stocks is necessary to properly diversify a portfolio.

SCHEDULE 13D. The required notification form filed with the Securities and Exchange Commission by a person or group who acquires more than five percent of a company's outstanding equity securities. Among the items included in the form are the identity and background of the acquirer, the amount and source of funds used to make the purchases and a general statement regarding the purpose of the transaction.

SCORCHED-EARTH DEFENSE. An attempt by a target company to make itself less attractive to an unwanted acquirer. Actions may include selling off prime assets and making acquisitions that use up excess cash.

SECONDARY MARKET. Market where previously issued securities trade such as the New York Stock Exchange.

SHARK REPELLENT CLAUSES. Amendments to a company's charter and/ or bylaws designed to discourage unwanted suitors.

SHORT AGAINST THE BOX. Investment strategy of selling short while holding a long position in the security.

SHORT SALE. Sale of a security not yet owned in order to capitalize on an anticipated market price drop.

SHORT SQUEEZE. Rapid price rise forcing investors to cover their short positions. This drives the security price up even higher, often squeezing even more short investors.

SHOW-STOPPER. A substantive violation of law by an acquirer which would justify an injunction against the offer.

SPECIAL SITUATION. An undervalued security with special circumstances such as management change, new product, technological breakthrough, etc., favoring its return to better operating performance and higher prices.

SPIN-OFF. Shedding of a corporate subsidiary, division or other operation via the issuance of shares in the new corporate entity.

SPLIT. A change in the number of outstanding shares through board of directors' action. Shareholder's equity remains the same, each shareholder receives the new stock in proportion to their holdings on the date of record. Dividends and earnings per share are adjusted to reflect the stock split.

SPREAD. The difference, either in dollars or as a percentage, between the current market price of the target company's securities and their expected value upon completion of the transaction.

S & P 500. A broad-based stock index composed of 400 industrial, 40 financial, 40 utility and 20 transportation stocks.

STANDSTILL AGREEMENT. A negotiated settlement between a target company and a potential unfriendly acquirer which sets a limit on the number of shares that the acquirer may purchase over a specified period of time.

STRIKING PRICE. The price at which an option or future contract can be executed according to the terms of the contract. Also called exercise price.

10K,10Q. Annual and quarterly reports required by the Securities and Exchange Commission. They contain more in-depth financial and operating information then the annual and quarterly stockholder's reports.

TARGET. The company that is the object of an acquisition proposal, tender offer, etc.

TECHNICAL ANALYSIS. Investment strategy that focuses on market and stock price patterns.

TOP-DOWN INVESTING. Investment strategy starting with the overall economic scenario and then moving downward to consider industry and individual company investments.

TOTAL RETURN. The return achieved by combining both the dividend/ interest and capital appreciation earned on an investment.

TRADING RANGE. The spread between the high and low prices for a given period.

TURNAROUND. A positive change in the fortunes of a company or industry. Turnarounds occur for a variety of reasons such as economic upturn, new management, new product lines, strategic acquisition, etc.

UNDERLYING SECURITY. The security which may be bought or sold under the terms of an option agreement, warrant, etc.

UNDERVALUED SITUATION. A security with a market value that does not fully value its potential or the true value of the company.

UPTREND. Upward movement in the market price of a stock.

VALUE AVERAGING. An investment purchase method that concentrates on the investment's value not its cost.

VENTURE CAPITAL. Funds provided by individuals or groups, as start- up or expansion capital, typically for an ownership percentage of the enterprise.

VOLUME. The number of units of a security traded during a given time frame.

WARRANT. An option to purchase a stated number of shares at a specified price within a specific time frame. Warrants are typically offered as sweeteners to enhance the marketability of stock or debt issues.

WHITE KNIGHT. A third party which, by offering a higher price in a friendly transaction, saves a target company from being acquired by an unwelcome bidder.

WORKING CAPITAL. The difference between current assets and current liabilities.

YIELD. An investment's return from its interest or dividend paying capability.

ZERO COUPON. A bond selling at a discount to maturity value and earning interest over the life of the bond but paying it upon maturity.

Index

AES Corporation, 73
ALLTEL Corporation , 65-66
AT&T Corporation, 137,149
Albemarle Corporation, 137
Aluminum Company of America, 76-77
Alward, Tim, 168
American depositary receipts, 76, 181
American International Group, Inc.,
    32-33,150,153
AmSouth Bancorporation, 25-26
Asquith, Krishna and Healy, 146

Babson-United Investment Advisors, Inc., 151
Baker Hughes Inc., 56-57
BankAmerica Corporation, 171
Bank of Boston, 26-27
Bank of New York Company, Inc., 28-29
Barnett Banks, Inc., 31
Baxter International, 137
Bay Networks, Inc., 66-67
Becton Dickinson, 45
Bed Bath & Beyond Inc., 153-154
Belden Inc., 47-48
Big B Inc., 73
Biogen, Inc., 45
Biomet, Inc., 171
Birinyi Associates, 169
Blecher, Katrina, 24

Boatman's Bancshares, 31
Boston Scientific, 45
Brown, Keith, C., 120-121
Buffet, Warren, 21, 99-100

CML Market Letter, 104
Cable Design Technologies, 72
Cadbury Schweppes PLC, 78-79
Campbell Soup Company, 74
Cardinal Health Inc. 38-40
Carson Pirie Scott, 74
Central and South West Corporation, 5, 79-80
Century Shares Trust, 13-15,38
Cheyenne Software, 72
Chrysler Corporation, 94,96,98,101
Claire's Stores, Inc., 155-156
Columbia/HCA Healthcare Corporation, 40-41
Commercial Metals Company, 172
Consolidated Papers, Inc. 57-59
Crane Company, 48-50
Cummings, Fred A., 24
Cusatis, Patrick J., 121

Deere & Company, 156-157
Dial Corporation, 137
Diodes Inc., 72
Disclosure, Inc., 22

193

Divining the Dow, 178-179
Dow Chemical Company, 59-60,172
Dun & Bradstreet Corporation 120, 130-132
Duriron Company, 50-51

Eastman Chemical Company, 132-133
Emerson Electric Company, 51-52,150-151
EnviroSource Inc., 107-108
Evans, Richard L., 95-96,99-100

FMC Corporation, 60-61
Fama, Fisher, Jensen and Roll, 146
Federal Home Loan Mortgage Corporation, 164,172,184
Federal National Mortgage Association, 33, 173
Fifth Third Bancorp, 31
First Bank System, Inc., 173
First Data Corporation, 24, 33-35
FiServ Inc., 24,35-36
Fleet Financial Group, 31
Ford Investor Services, Inc., 147-148,168-169
Forest City Enterprises Inc., 173
Freeport-McMoRan Copper & Gold, 126
Freeport-McMoRan Inc., 125-126, 148
Freeport-McMoRan Resource Partners, LP, 126
Frontier Corporation, 68-69
Fulkerson, Allan W. 13-15

Gaming & Investments Quarterly, 179
General Electric Company, 174
Geon Company, 134-135
Georgia-Pacific Corporation, 62-63,151-152
Glaxco-Wellcome PLC, 81-82
Goodstein, Barbara, 138
Gradison-McDonald Asset Management, 101,124,145
Green, Frederick W., 4, 21
Gruntal & Company, Inc., 24

Healthsouth Corporation, 45
Hewlett-Packard Company, 72
H & R Block, 137
Hancock (John) Regional Bank Fund, 11-13,38
Harlow, Van, 121
Hometown Investor, The, 178-179
Hong Kong Telecommunications Ltd., 82-83
Huntington Bancshares, 31

Iacocca, Lee, 98,101
Ikenberry, David, 147,167-168
Ikenberry, Lakonishok and Vermaelen, 167-168
Ikenberry, Rankine and Stice, 147
Investment Counselors of Maryland, 73,166

Johnson & Johnson, 5,42-43

Kerkorian, Kirk, 94
Kimberly-Clark Corporation, 5,63-64

LaLoggia, Charles M., 104,126-127
LaLoggia's Special Situation Report and Stock Market Forecast, 104,126
Laidlaw Inc., 108-109
Landstar System Inc., 74
Lexmark International, 137
Liberty Bancorp, Inc., 31
Logicon, Inc., 174
Luxottica Group SpA, 5,84-85

McDonald & Company Securities, Inc., 24
Main Street Beats Wall Street, 178-179
Manpower Inc., 74
Mattel, Inc., 157-158
Measurex Corporation, 69-70
Melville Corporation, 137
Merck & Company, 43,149,164, 175
Merger Fund, The, 4,7-8,21
Mergers and acquisitions, 3-89
Mikkelson, Wayne, 20-21
Miles, James A., 121
Minnesota Mining & Manufacturing, 137
Money Making Investments 178-179
Mutual Beacon, 9-11

NationsBank Corporation, 29-30
Neuhauser, Charles, 73-74,166
New Generation Research, Inc., 104
New York Stock Exchange Fact Book, 141-142,150
North American Biologicals, 45

105 Best Investments for the Twenty-First Century, 178-179
Old Kent Financial, 31
Ohlson and Penman, 146
Omnicom Group, Inc., 74
OrthoLogic, 45

194

PacifiCorp, 85-86
Park Electrochemical Corporation, 71-72
Paychex, Inc., 74
Penederm Inc., 45
Pep Boys-Manny Moe & Jack, 74
Pfizer, Inc., 43-45,149
Phelps Dodge Corporation, 94-96,164
Praxair, Inc., 53-54
Premark International, 138
Price, Michael, 9-11
Putnam III, George, 105-106, 138

RPM, Inc., 159-160
Reilly and Drzycimski, 146
ReliaStar Financial Corporation, 36-37
Reynolds & Reynolds Company, 175
Rothchild Inc., 139
Ruback, Richard, 20-21

St. Jude Medical, 46
Sanifill, Inc., 110-111
Schmidt, John, 11-12
Schulman A., Inc., 175-176
Securities Data Company, 1, 119, 163
Sensormatic Electronics Corporation, 111-112
Seyhun, H. Nejat, 152
Sherwin Williams, 5, 75
Simon & Company, Charles E., 22
Smith International, Inc., 113-114
Spin-off Monitor, 139
Spin-off Report, 139
Spin-offs, 119-139
Sprint Corporation, 138
Standex International Corporation, 176
Staples, Inc., 75
Staton, Bill, 131-132,174
Staton Institute for America's Finest Investors,
    132
Stock buybacks, 163-177
Stock Picking, 178-179
Stock splits, 141-161
Stovall, Robert, 144-145,149-150
Stovall/Twenty-First Advisers Inc., 145
Structural Dynamics Research Corporation,
    114-115
Sun Gard Data Systems, 73

21st Century Investments, 179
Tele Danmark, 86-87

Thermo Instrument Systems Inc., 135-136
Third Avenue Value Fund, Inc., 15-18
Toro Company, 75
Transport Holdings, 138
TransTexas Gas Corporation, 116-117
Trans World Airlines, Inc., 105-106
Turnaround Letter, The, 104-105
Turnarounds, 93-118
Turner, Bradley E., 101, 124, 145

Uniforce Temporary Personnel, Inc., 177
Unilever N.V., 5,87-89,150
Utilites & Energy Portfolio, 178-179
United & Babson Investment Report, 151
United Healthcare, 46
U.S. Bancorp, 31
United States Filter Corporation, 54-55
United Stationers, 75
Union Pacific, 5, 75

Vanourek, R., 112
Vectra Banking, 31
Victoria Bankshares, 31

WMS Industries, 127
Walter, Robert, D. 39
West Coast Bancorp, 31
Whitman, Martin J., 15-18
Woolridge, J. Randall, 121-123

Zangwill, Willard, I. 6
Zions Bancorporation, 32

Investment
Advertisement
Offers

The following investment advertisements are presented for your convenience. While their inclusion is not meant as an endorsement, it is our hope that they prove informative and beneficial to your investment performance.

197

Featured in Richard J. Maturi's
The 105 Best Investments for the 21st Century

WELLS
REAL ESTATE FUNDS

> *"Out of 150 real estate sponsors who exhibited at the 1985 International Association for Financial Planning Convention, only one was still exhibiting at the 1992 and 1993 conventions, Wells Real Estate Funds."*
>
> Richard J. Maturi,
> **The 105 Best Investments
> for the 21st Century**

For more information, contact your financial advisor
or call Wells Real Estate Funds at 800-448-1010.

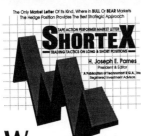

How to

Take the Guesswork
Out of Investing

HERE'S HOW: Invest exclusively in the 30 Dow Jones stocks, such as DuPont, J.P. Morgan, Coca-Cola, Boeing, Disney, Proctor & Gamble, General Electric...and 23 other blue chip stocks.

THE REASON THIS IDEA WORKS: The Dow Jones Industrial Average is the benchmark that everyone uses to gauge how they're doing. For some strange reason, however, most people fail to do as well as the Dow. This includes mutual funds, bank trust departments, pension plans and other professionals.

The Advantages

☞ **Simplicity.** Buy equal dollar amounts of each stock.

☞ **Low commissions,** since the only time you sell is when a stock is replaced in the Dow — about one stock a year. You can even use dividend reinvestment plans (DRIPs) to further reduce commissions. Only 5 Dow stocks don't have a (DRIP).

☞ **Low Capital Gains Taxes,** since you rarely sell.

☞ **No decisions to make.** It's all automatic.

☞ **No studying or reading** is necessary.

How to Beat the Market

If you could **select the best 10** of these 30 stocks and emphasize them by investing 4% in each — and only 3% in each of the remaining 20, **you would automatically beat the market** year after year.

TO FIND OUT HOW, read one of my books: *Safe Investing* (Simon & Schuster, 1991) or *Straight Talk About Stock Investing* (McGraw-Hill, 1995). Or, contact me for further information.

JOHN SLATTER, CFA
Senior Portfolio Strategist

RM Investment Management
70 Beech Street, Essex Junction, Vermont 05452
Call toll-free (888) 872-0637

Investment Newsletters

Utility & Energy Portfolio (quarterly)   Covers the changing utility and energy industry; EVERY BUY/SELL RECOMMENDATION A WINNER SINCE INCEPTION OF NEWSLETTER IN 1992; WorldCom up 60%, Southwest Energy up 30%, Cincinnati Bell Up 25%

21st Century Investments (quarterly)   Provides regular updates on investments in "The 105 Best Investments for the 21st Century" and other stocks poised to outperform into the next century; Danka Business Systems up 50%, St. Jude Medical up 40%, Reynolds & Reynolds up 36%.

Gaming & Investments Quarterly   Ferrets out unique investments in the explosive gaming, recreation, leisure industry; Caesars World 34% gain, Caesars World short sale 21% gain, Casino America 42% gain, Sodak Gaming 74% gain.

Utility & Energy Portfolio ($95/yr)	35.00
21st Century Inv. ($95/yr) intro price	15.00
Gaming & Investments Quarterly ($75/yr)	25.00

See order information on pages 178-179

Selected Small Cap Stocks Are Exploding!

Is it time to buy, sell, or hold? Most analysts haven't a clue! For your clues, consult noted financial analyst Kenneth Coleman. Ken's two newsletters, *21 Small Cap Stocks* and *The Fed Tracker*, publish timely buy, sell, & hold recommendations on the hottest growh companies. What returns are possible in small cap investing with Ken Coleman? Here's a partial list of the 1995 percentage of increase for stocks recommended by *21 Small Cap Stocks*:

Adaptec	ADPT	135%	Comdisco	CDO	135%
ADC Telecom	ADCT	115%	Olsten Corp.	OLS	131%
Cal Micro	CMIC	265%	Teradyne	TER	426%

Here's a partial list of the hard asset sector stocks and their percentage of increase since recommendation (Chase and Metallica recommended in 1st Quarter 1996):

Allegheny Mines	AYM.A	92%	Corriente Res.	CTQ.V	125%
Yuma Mines	YUM.V	80%	Guyana Gold	GUY.V	100%
Chase Res. Corp.	OQS.V	31%	Metallica Res.	MR.T	33%

Ken hasn't lost a dime for subscribers in the hard asset sector since 1991. The reason is simple: Money Flow Analysis. It provides the accurate timing points to switch in and out of different investment sectors. The stock market is correcting sector to sector. Have you been making these kinds of profits? Call Jeff Taylor at London Taylor Communications for a free copy of Ken's newsletters & updates on Ken's hard asset analysis. Phone (800) 485-0108, San Diego residents call (619) 431-5135.

Making Money With M&A? Make More - Offshore

LIKE INSIDER TRADING
WITHOUT ALL THAT
UNPLEASANT JAIL TIME.

WHILE WE soundly condemn the practice of insider trading, we understand a few of the reasons it appeals to certain rascally investors.

In a way, you want what they want. To get the best information. To catch the next rising star. To profit from your investments. Significantly.

Fortunately, as a law-abiding investor, you have an alternative. A subscription to *The Red Chip Review*.

We're an investment resource. And our sole purpose is to introduce you to stocks that should trounce the market.

We succeed by finding promising companies long before they show up on Wall Street's radar. They're often small. Underfollowed. Undervalued. Yet they have breakthrough ideas. Great stories. A hungry spirit. And they fill unique niches.

Plus, we cover only companies whose management establishes a candid relationship with our analysts. That way, as soon as they can share information with us, we can pass it along to you.

So far, only 288 companies have made it through our screens. And their performance has been remarkable.

In 1995, these "Red Chip" stocks had an average return of 46%. Our top 100 averaged 135%. Our #1 pick, Iomega, showed a one-year gain of 1396%.

This year, the biggest gainers will probably be different companies. But the big question is, which ones?

For more information, call us. We'll send you a helpful booklet containing a sample *Red Chip* report. The names of 1995's top 50 performers. Our philosophy for choosing stocks. And much more.

One year of the *Red Chip Review* — 24 issues — is just $349. You can also get our information in other ways, according to your needs. From single reports downloaded from our World Wide Web site, to a one-year subscription including timely fax updates. We can offer the choice, and the price, that's right for you.

If you want an outstanding guide to up-and-coming stocks, you won't be able to do any better. Legally, anyway.

{ *One Year (24 issues)~$349*
800.721.1972 }

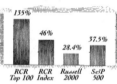

Red Chip Review Stocks:
Outstanding Performance in 1995

135%   46%   37.5%   28.4%
RCR   RCR   Russell   S&P
Top 100 Index   2000   500

THE RED CHIP REVIEW
The unbiased word on small-cap stocks.

For a free booklet, call 1-800-721-1972 (7 am-5 pm PST). Or http://www.redchip.com

Do Your Friends and Colleagues a Favor by Giving Them a FREE Copy of "Bill Staton's WealthBuilding Advisory".

So many people have benefited from the valuable insights and advice that's contained in each monthly issue of "Bill Staton's WealthBuilding Advisory" you will be doing your friends, relatives and colleagues – and yourself – a real favor if you send us their names so we can mail a no-obligation sample issue. It will be sent FREE with your compliments.

And, "yes" we will be glad to send you a FREE copy of this newsletter so you can see for yourself just how useful Bill Staton's plain-English advice can be. There's no limit to the number of names you can send us. Just be sure you submit a complete address in a legible way.

Your Name *(please print)* _____

Address _____

City/State/ZIP _____

Daytime Phone _____ Fax _____

Initial here _____ if you want a no-obligation free sample issue of "WBA" for yourself. Write below how you want each "gift notice" to read:

From: _____

At no-obligation, send FREE sample issue of "WealthBuilding Advisory" newsletter to:

Name _____

Address _____

City/State/ZIP _____

NOTE: *If you wish to send additional names and addresses please feel free to photocopy this form or simply submit separate sheet(s) of paper. Mail to "Sample Newsletter" c/o The Staton Institute for America's Finest Investors, 300 East Blvd. B-4, Charlotte, NC 28203.*

205